MULTI-GENERATIONAL FAMILY THERAPY

D1555160

Multi-generational Family Therapy reveals the limits of the medical model in treating mental and relational problems. It instead provides a toolkit for therapists, observing family functioning over at least three generations to explore the developmental history of the family in order to discover links between past trauma and broken emotional bonds, and current problems experienced by family members. Maurizio Andolfi honours the voices of children in therapy and enlists them as the key to unlocking unresolved family issues.

The book provides an experiential model of intervention that centres on creativity and humanity as the best way to build an alliance and work with a family in crisis. Demonstrating with case examples, Andolfi outlines the relational skills and inner self of the therapist, focusing on the ability to be direct, authentic and empathic. The use of relational questioning, silence, body language, physical contact and movement in therapy is explored in depth.

Multi-generational Family Therapy will be of interest to anyone working with individuals, couples and families, including child, adolescent and adult psychotherapists, psychiatrists, psychologists and counsellors. It will also prove useful to private practitioners, social workers, doctors, paediatricians and educators.

Maurizio Andolfi, MD, is a child psychiatrist and a world-renowned master family therapist. He was Professor in Clinical Psychology at the University la Sapienza, Rome, and co-founder of the European Family Therapy Association, and is currently Director of the Accademia di Psicoterapia della Famiglia Rome. Andolfi is editor of the journal *Terapia Familiare* and has previously published many books, including *Please, Help Me with This Family* (Routledge, 1994). In 2016, Andolfi received the Life Achievement award from the American Family Therapy Academy.

MULTI-GENERATIONAL FAMILY THERAPY

Tools and Resources for the Therapist

Maurizio Andolfi

Routledge
Taylor & Francis Group

LONDON AND NEW YORK

First published 2017
by Routledge
2 Park Square, Milton Park, Abingdon, Oxon OX14 4RN

and by Routledge
711 Third Avenue, New York, NY 10017

Routledge is an imprint of the Taylor & Francis Group, an informa business

British Library Cataloguing in Publication Data
A catalogue record for this book is available from the British Library

Library of Congress Cataloging in Publication Data
Names: Andolfi, Maurizio.
Title: Multi-generational family therapy : tools and resources for
    the therapist / Maurizio Andolfi.
Description: London ; New York : Routledge, 2017. | Includes
    bibliographical references.
Identifiers: LCCN 2016011993 | ISBN 9781138670969 (hbk) |
    ISBN 9781138670976 (pbk) | ISBN 9781315545592 (ebk)
Subjects: LCSH: Family psychotherapy.
Classification: LCC RC488.5 .A4818 2017 | DDC 616.89/
    156—dc23
LC record available at https://lccn.loc.gov/2016011993

ISBN: 978-1-138-67096-9 (hbk)
ISBN: 978-1-138-67097-6 (pbk)
ISBN: 978-1-315-54559-2 (ebk)

Typeset in Bembo
by Swales & Willis Ltd, Exeter, Devon, UK

To my son Jonathan, who helps me to stay young

CONTENTS

Acknowledgements   *x*
Introduction   *xi*

1 The roots of Relational Psychology   1
   The origins of Systems Theory 1
   Systems and Multigenerational Theories: two models compared 3
   The system purists and the conductors 5
   On the inter-subjectivity of observation 6

2 The family life cycle and the multi-generational dimension   9
   The family life cycle theory 9
   Multi-generational family narrative 11
   Invisible loyalties 12
   The conquest of personal authority 13
   Family myths as an expression and vehicle for family culture 14
   The differentiation of self 17
   Emotional cut-off 18
   Inter-generational intimidation and the chronic child 19

3 Social transformation and new family forms   24
   Children of divorced and single-parent families 25
   Step-parenting and blended families 26
   Single-person families 28
   De facto relationships and families 28
   Adoptive families 29

Cross-cultural and immigrant families 31
Homosexual couples and children of same-sex parents 34

4 Family observation methods   39
The triad as a basic unit of observation 39
The genogram: a graphic representation of family development 42
How to use the genogram in therapy and consultation 44
How to use the genogram in training therapists 46
Family sculpture: a powerful tool for systemic therapists 47
Family sculpture in therapy 48
*Sculpting in supervision and in the personal training of the
    therapist 50*
Role-playing in therapy and training 52

5 Toward an assessment of family functioning   56
The three-storey house 56
Difference in couple's configurations 57
The harmonious couple 58
The high-conflict couple 58
The unstable couple 59
The "sandwiched" couple, caught between two generations 59
Social assessment of couple functioning 60
*The birth of the child: a major transformation in a couple's
    relationship 61*
The assessment of the sibling relationship 63

6 The construction of the therapeutic story   66
The formation of a therapeutic alliance with the family 66
The child as co-therapist 68
The inner self of the therapist and self-disclosure 69
The relational skills of the family therapist 71
Rituals and dramatization in family therapy 78

7 The language of the therapeutic encounter   82
The foundations of the therapeutic dialogue 83
Gathering and selection of information 85
Reframing and relational statements 86
Relational questions 89

8 Body language in family therapy   96
Eye language and facial expressions 97
Gestures and body signals 98
Body spacing and relational boundaries 99

Physical contact 100
The paralinguistic system and silence 100
How to use the eyes in family therapy 101
The movement in therapeutic space 104
Movement in the formation of therapeutic alliance 106

9 Silence and touch: two powerful ways to connect   111
Pauses of reflection 111
The significance of silence of the family and of the
     therapist 112
Silence as a support to family grief 114
Touching: physical contact in family therapy 116
Physical contact: a positive reinforcement of the therapeutic
     alliance 119
Physical contact to rebuild connections 121
Case example: Rob's burdens 124

10 The human dimension in psychotherapy and research   131
The limit of the medical model in treating mental and relational
     problems 131
Research on the effectiveness of family therapy 132
An attempt to include families in long-term follow-up clinical
     research 134
The recovery of Thomas: a miracle or a healing therapeutic
     process? 136

Index   *141*

ACKNOWLEDGEMENTS

I would like to thank two dear friends and family therapists, Chiara Hunter, for her translation of the entire manuscript into English, and Narina Sidhu, for a very professional and scholarly revision and editing of the book. I thank Anna Mascellani for her critical comments and valuable observations about the text, and Laura Bruno for helping me to compile the bibliography. Lastly, special thanks to my wife, Lorena, for her suggestions regarding the structure and content of this work and her technological assistance. But, even more so for her "home support" over a year, the time it took me to write this volume, between professional engagements and long, inspiring walks along the beautiful coastline of City Beach, in Perth.

INTRODUCTION

This volume is the result of 45 years of international therapeutic experience in my work with families and couples around the world, often in the role of therapist and at other times as consultant or supervisor. This wealth of transcultural experiences has helped me to appreciate values, traditions and expressions of affection and care, which have enriched my own familial and social roots, a real heritage of knowledge and understanding of family life. I learnt family therapy by personally observing master therapists at work and absorbing their skills and knowledge. As one does when learning a trade, we gather knowledge by observation and "steal with our eyes", as an old Italian saying goes! I have tried to keep this tradition alive by presenting my work with families through either live consultations or supervisions, or showing taped sessions with clients. Whatever I have learned over the years I have tried to give back to the scientific community by demonstrating my own innovative way of doing therapy. I am afraid that family therapy that is learned, practised and demonstrated through experiential work, passed from one generation to another, is in danger of disappearing. Nowadays, teachers at universities and conferences tend to hide behind theories that illustrate different models and approaches, and descriptions of their own clinical interventions, rather than showcase personal demonstrations of their work.

These sentiments are echoed by Minuchin, one of my greatest teachers, in the introduction to his latest book, *The Craft of Family Therapy* (Minuchin, Reiter & Borda, 2014). Minuchin describes how university programmes nowadays operate principally through a *deductive method*, where students learn various family therapy theories and then attempt to apply them in practice. Through this method, they learn to be measured, protective and detached from emotional discomfort and personal involvement with the client's pain. In essence, they are programmed to move cautiously and to avoid superimposing a personal frame of reference on the family's problems. Thus, the student is not encouraged to look at herself as a resource when practising therapy or to explore a more *inductive* learning process based on doing and on the experiential work with families.

This book draws on the concepts of Relational Psychology (Andolfi, 2003), a new and fascinating discipline that utilizes the triad as a unit of measure of interpersonal relationships in the developmental history of families. I hope this method will take root and flourish, and make a vital contribution to currently popular disciplines, such as Dynamic Psychology and Cognitive Psychology, which are, in contrast, strongly anchored in individual therapy. This will encourage new clinical research on the primary triangle, where the father's role is honoured and, more generally, on all observational models of child development. Systemic theories opened a new territory in the observation of human relationships, but without a study into the evolutionary dynamics of the family over generations, the observation of family interactions in "the here and now" only provides a group picture, without a past or future perspective.

In this observation of the family spanning several generations, an important role is given to the subsystem of the children, who are engaged in therapy as significant relational bridges in the dialogue or clash between generations. This active role of children and adolescents in therapy, especially when they are the bearers of symptomatic behaviours, is without doubt the most original aspect of my clinical experience and of the multigenerational family therapy model proposed in this volume. Having noticed the limitations and often the damage caused by the widespread pharmacological treatment of many types of child and adolescent psychopathology, over time, I developed the conviction that *the family is the best medicine*. The cure, therefore, consists of revisiting together the family's developmental history, stitching up still open wounds and healing broken emotional bonds. The presenting problem becomes an access door to the family's world and the identified patient, a privileged guide in the exploration of family ties. The first concrete result of this therapeutic proposal will be the gradual disappearance of symptoms in the person for whom intervention was required, but even more significant, will be to observe the affective and relational transformation between family members, both on the couple dimension and on the intergenerational relationships. The family will thus move from a passive position of delegating to the expert, typical of a medical model, to a leading role in its own destiny, within the kind of therapy that helps it to discover its own resources rather than highlighting its failures.

For this to happen, it is necessary for the therapist to keep in mind a multigenerational map of the family that he meets in therapy, a kind of "living genogram", where he can access active resources and open healing pathways. The therapist needs to adopt the curiosity of an explorer who enters into the private world of each family, while remaining centred. This volume provides the identikit for such a therapist and highlights her cognitive and affective qualities within the therapeutic experience with families and couples. Her professional toolkit consists of multiple instruments designed to promote a trusting and cooperative therapeutic relationship with each family member. It is necessary to develop a creative repertoire of relational questions and to listen attentively to each person's voice, honouring adults as well as children. At the same time, it is important during the session to be able to grasp those non-verbal signals transmitted by the body, the eyes, by gestures and posture that are more eloquent than words, and to appreciate pauses and silences rich in relational meanings.

The therapist we are describing should be free from cultural stereotypes and institutional routines, to be able to use herself, her affective resonance and the therapeutic space in an active way, approaching and establishing physical contact with this or that family member, facilitating new connections and mending the emotional disconnections of the past. Her physical and internal presence, besides the professional one, is the most effective therapeutic instrument to make direct and authentic contact with each person, by attuning to the pain and desperation expressed by many families in therapy, as well as to the implicit aspects of vitality and hope, in order to transform them into elements of strength and change.

Nowadays, the forms that the family takes are many and varied and reflect the profound transformations of contemporary society. They are different from each other and from the traditional family, but the evolutionary matrix and intergenerational reading of the history can become a common and, in many ways, universal guide. This transformative operation of the meaning itself of therapeutic intervention requires the therapist to be able to enter with passion and empathy into even the most difficult and dramatic issues of the family without a judgemental or classificatory attitude.

References

Andolfi, M. (2003). *Manuale di Psicologia Relazionale*. Rome: A.P.F.
Minuchin, S., Reiter, M. D. & Borda, C. (2014). *The Craft of Family Therapy: Challenging Certainties*. New York: Routledge.

1

THE ROOTS OF RELATIONAL PSYCHOLOGY

The origins of Systems Theory

Relational Psychology finds its roots in the American culture of the 1950s, characterized by an attempt to overcome the fragmentation of isolated studies and interventions with the introduction of a holistic model to deal with people's problems. Such a new interdisciplinary approach provided fertile ground for the development of social sciences like anthropology and sociology, which offered a significant contribution to the understanding of the socio-cultural contexts in the individual's life cycle, as well as the influence of family dynamics on personality development. In particular, in the field of psychology, *Neo-Freudian theories* brought about a radical shift from observing mostly intra-psychic factors, to exploring inter-personal phenomena and the cultural and social contexts in which they take place. In the opening session of an outstanding International Conference on The Pioneers of Family Therapy, held in Rome in 2000, Minuchin stated that the Neo-Freudian group formed by Sullivan, Fromm, Horney and Thompson were the real precursors of the incipient movement of family therapy.

From this theoretical framework, Systems Theory emerged. It represents the structure that connects (Bateson, 1979) the various fields of understanding (from mathematics to natural history to humanities), and is based upon such concepts as systems, organization, self-regulation, totality and circular causality. The *General Systems Theory*, introduced by the biologist Von Bertalanffy, was systematically organized in 1968. The focus of interest for the observer changed from isolated phenomena to "organized wholes". Such a vision of reality introduced a new language and an innovative scientific lexicon applicable to the study of any system: live organisms, social organizations, computers and human systems. The systemic perspective adopted a wide-angle lens: it looked at the world in terms of the inter-dependence and inter-relationship of all observed phenomena and this integrated reference scheme, whose properties cannot be reduced to those of its parts, was designated a *system* (Capra, 1982). In this sense, this model allowed the observer to isolate the characteristics common to all systems, understood as whole, intelligent units interacting amongst themselves (Miller, 1978).

The introduction of a systemic-cybernetic perspective to family studies is due to Palo Alto's Mental Research Institute, represented by Watzlawick, Jackson, Haley and Weakland, among others. These authors were the direct followers of the Batesonian ideas and borrowed concepts and language from communication theories in animals and machines (input and output, feedback, etc.). The access key to the family, seen as a self-correcting system with stable connections tending to homeostasis, is provided by the psychic discomfort in the individual, which in turn translates into a distortion in communication. They were responsible for theorizing that families are organized by a tendency to maintain the status quo (homeostasis), with particular rules of communication and more or less rigid sets of interactions. The model proposed by the group focused on observable aspects of behaviour/communication in the *here and now,* that is to say, on the interactive dimension. They attempted to connect a particular type of communication with a specific symptomatology, which led them to develop ways of assisting people to communicate better.

In the mid-1950s, the *Double-bind Theory* (Bateson, Jackson, Haley & Weakland, 1956) provided a theoretical framework for understanding and treating dysfunctional forms of communication typical of dyadic relationships. Such a concept derived from an attempt at explaining major psychiatric dysfunctions, primarily schizophrenia, in terms of causal circularity and therefore connected to particular types of interaction between different family members. Various authors criticized this idea for remaining trapped in mechanistic concepts of linear causality, in a search for the ultimate causes of symptoms (Minuchin, 1974, 2002; Ugazio, 1985; Telfener, 2002; Andolfi & Mascellani, 2013). In effect, even though they worked in collaboration with Bateson and shared with him an ambitious research project on various forms of communication, the group did not understand the complexity of his concept, and were unable to free themselves from the mechanistic model they were attempting to overcome. Aetiology (the search for the cause), typical of the Medical Model, continued to guide family studies. This gave rise to the dyadic theory that dysfunctional communication between two individuals who are emotionally bonded leads inevitably to the manifestation of pathology, when one person is unable to decipher the contradictory messages given by the other. An example of double bind is highlighted by the dysfunctional communication between a mother and child, where the mother tells the child, "I love you", whilst her intonation and body language demonstrate the opposite, and the child is unable to make sense of the contradiction. In reality, the Double-bind Theory, as an explanation of major psychiatric disorders, was an interesting research idea, but when applied to clinical practice it resulted in total failure and was strongly opposed by the families associated with the National Alliance on Mental Illness (NAMI) in the United States, because it was considered judgemental and accusatory towards the parents of schizophrenic patients.

The decline of this theoretic model was highlighted in 1978 during a conference held in New York, entitled "Beyond the Double Bind Theory". A book by the same title was published later that year (Berger, 1978).

The axioms of human communication, including a thorough exploration of verbal and non-verbal language, and the difference between content and context are described in the well-known book, *Pragmatics of Human Communication* (Watzlavick, Beavin & Jackson, 1967). This book provides very useful guidelines to orient therapists in working with clients. The adoption of a systemic-cybernetic perspective opened a critical debate on the monadic vision of the individual, a prisoner of his inner world, contrasting it with the view of an individual as a social being, whose behaviour can be understood within the context of the relational system he inhabits. The communicational features of every event and action, including symptomatic behaviour, are highlighted by this approach. An individual's problem is viewed also as a signal of the relational discomfort in the family, and communicates the existence of conflict between homeostasis and change.

To summarize, Systems Theory is based on looking at the family as an organized system. Every behaviour is understood as a function of the relationship according to the context within which interactions take place. The focus of interest shifts from the idea of an artificially isolated individual to the relationships between the dynamics of the larger family system. The idea of context in the study of family relationships is a key point of the model proposed by Watzlawick et al. (1967). Devoid of context, words and actions have no meaning. Context is defined not only by the words that are spoken, but also by the non-verbal communication, which are mutually reinforcing and constantly evolving. The presenting issue can thus be viewed in another light, in that it is no longer considered solely as the manifestation of individual discomfort or illness, but highlights the dysfunction within the family system. Haley (1976) made another significant contribution. He proposed the triad as the basic unit of observation of relational phenomena, an innovative idea that allowed the therapist to look at family interactions through a new lens and to adopt different ways of gathering information, which later was described as "circular questioning". His finding of *perverse triads* in the presence of severe individual symptoms led him, in the late 1960s, to open himself up to new influences, firstly through the strategic approach of hypnosis by Milton Erickson and later through Minuchin's *Structural Theory* (1972).

Systems and Multi-generational Theories: two models compared

The development of Systems Theory did not lead to the definition of a common conceptual and operative model to look at family functioning and individual psychopathology. Since the 1960s, two different schools of thought in the area of family studies began to take shape and confront each other. On the west coast of the United States, the Palo Alto group studied the first axioms of human communication (which would culminate in the Double-bind Theory). On the east coast, another group formed that came from a psychodynamic tradition. Principally represented by Bowen, Boszormenyi-Nagy, Framo, Whitaker and, at some level, by Minuchin and his structural school, their work was fundamental in orienting the focus towards a developmental perspective that took into account the individual's development within the family's life cycle.

Pragmatics of human communication

The theoretical formulations of the systemic movement (Watzlawick et al., 1967; Selvini Palazzoli, Boscolo, Cecchin & Prata, 1978; Haley & Hoffman, 1981) were focused mainly on the observable communications and interactions in the family system taking place in the here and now, without connecting them to the developmental process of which they are a part. The observed reality was imprisoned in a static way: the natural formulation of a system and its development over time was reduced to a single dimension, the present. The limitation in such a vision was to consider the individual's subjectivity as a "black box" that trapped his thoughts, emotions, motivations, expectations, imagination and meaning. This reduced observation exclusively to pragmatic aspects, ignoring temporal aspects made up of a past, a present and a future and a whole world of meaning. In spite of the limiting exclusion of the family's historical and subjective aspects, the communicational theory gave the opportunity to contrast the dominant ideas of that period, and acquired an autonomous identity in relation to a strong psychoanalytic tradition that was based on verbal discourse and on the intra-psychic dynamics in the individual.

It is important to note that the group comprising Watzlawick, Beavin, Fish and Weakland, who worked for almost 30 years at the Mental Research Institute in Palo Alto, was mainly interested in brief individual interventions with a strategic orientation. In spite of this, *Pragmatics of Human Communication* (Watzlawick et al., 1967) became the family therapist's bible for at least two decades, particularly in Europe, perhaps because of its strong opposition to a firmly rooted and dominant psychoanalytic tradition. During the 1970s, the group, headed by Selvini Palazzoli in Milan, was inspired by Watzlawick's work and by the so-called "system purists," who insisted that the therapist had to maintain a neutral stance, with no emotional response to the clients' problems. Influenced by this, Selvini Palazzoli and her group wrote a classic article on how to conduct a session, which was based on three principal guidelines: the therapist's neutrality, the formulation of relational hypotheses and the use of circular questioning, devoid of any personal involvement of the therapist (Selvini Palazzoli, Boscolo, Cecchin & Prata, 1980).

The individual in the family

Multi-generational family therapy transforms ideas about the individual from the psychoanalytic approach and "the whole" from the systemic perspectives, to propose a new model that focuses on the individual within the larger system of the family and community. The foundation of multi-generational family therapy married ideas from several pioneers of the field – Bowen's concepts of the differentiation of self from the family of origin and the transmission of inter-generational immaturity (Bowen, 1978); Boszormenyi-Nagy and Spark's (1973) notion of invisible loyalties and inter-generational debits and credits; Framo's inter-generational approach to couple work (Framo, 1992; Framo, Weber & Levine, 2003); Whitaker's (1989) study of family myths and temporal jumps. Significantly, Whitaker became the most coherent and creative interpreter of the widening of relational interventions to include at least three generations. Minuchin's (1974) descriptions of enmeshed and disengaged families, which became fundamental in understanding child development in terms of history and boundaries between generations, were also included. Particular mention is due to the pioneering work of Ackerman (1958), who provided the most original relational interpretation of childhood symptoms and his idea of the symptomatic child as the scapegoat in family conflicts, using the primary triad as a model of observation and intervention in family dynamics.

None of these master therapists would define themselves purely as systemic, even though all had a knowledge of Von Bertalanffy's (1968) Systems Theory, Bateson's interdisciplinary approach (1979), and Watzlawick et al.'s (1967) axioms of human communication. Minuchin (2002) wrote an article published in the book *I Pionieri della Terapia Familiare* (Andolfi, 2002) regarding the importance of paying attention to people's cultural background. In this, he offered a critique on the systemic-cybernetic perspective. He said that Bateson's work, which inspired the systems theorists, oriented the clinician towards description rather than prescription, and towards ideas and away from people and their emotions. The seminal volume *Intensive Family Therapy*, edited by Boszormenyi-Nagy and Framo (1965), became a manifesto of multi-generational family therapy. These pioneers and their followers, even though they differed in many ways in terms of both theory and intervention, were aware that working with families meant meeting different family configurations, but always with a fundamental attention to the study of the individual in his growth process within the family. The family genogram introduced by Bowen (1978) became the tri-generational map, still used by therapists all over the world, by which to formulate a relational assessment of the family, noting significant events such as births, deaths, marriages and separations, useful in structuring treatment plans. For these authors, the individual would never be neglected or underestimated. Rather, the individual was encouraged either to repair emotional disconnections and to reconnect or to differentiate from inter-generational over-dependence. Above all, the goal of these pioneers was not merely to fix presenting problems, but more to understand the relational value of individual symptoms and, together with the family, to look for pathways to healing.

The system purists and the conductors

The outlining of such perspectives in family studies allowed the emergence of fundamental differences pertaining specifically to the consideration of presenting problems in the family, as well as to the role and function of the therapist. This influenced the basic objective of therapy: to observe interactions in the here and now and help clients to modify problematic behaviours, or assess behaviour and interactions to understand better emotions, expectations and motivation to change. Haley, in his farewell paper as Editor of *Family Process* (1969), outlined this divergence. On the one hand, we had the "system purists" like Watzlawick, Weakland, Hoffman and the Milan school, who studied the family as a system of interactions, placing themselves at a relative distance from any personal involvement and/or emotive resonance, using mainly a cognitive approach in therapy. On the other hand, we had the "conductors", those practitioners like Ackerman, Satir, Bowen, Framo, Minuchin, Whitaker and Andolfi, who used their own personality, including their emotional responses, as well as intuition and creativity, as instruments for creating a therapeutic alliance with the family and for guiding their interventions. In this sense, they elicited the creation of a third planet, to use a metaphor described by Andolfi and Angelo (1988), a therapeutic space shared with the family that fostered everyone's growth and self-knowledge. Their approach was essentially experiential in nature, designed to search for individual and relational resources capable of resolving the problems brought to therapy by the family.

On the inter-subjectivity of observation

During the past 50 years, there has been an evolution of systemic theories, especially in the transition from first- to second-order cybernetics. This has facilitated a more rounded view of the circularity of human communication. The promoters of the first-order cybernetic have often referred to *black boxes* (limited to the examination of *input and output* and its reverse process, *output and input*), focused on the observable aspects of interactive behaviour, viewing the observer as external to the observed. But the passage to second-order cybernetics, with the rise of *constructivism and social constructionism* (Mc Namee & Gergen, 1992), and the practice of *collaborative therapies* (Anderson & Goolishian, 1988), inaugurated a radical shift in how to view reality: then the client became the expert and therapy was considered a social construction with the therapist assuming a "not knowing" approach. The observer became part of the observed system and a new method of observation was thus set in motion; by placing the relationship between observers and observed at the forefront, the concepts of objectivity and of certainty appeared as illusory, allowing for the discovery of the subjective dimension of knowledge (Bocchi & Ceruti, 1985; Ceruti, 1994).

In his book *Observing Systems,* Von Foerster (1981), an outstanding constructivist theorist, underlines the importance of the subjectivity of the observer in the system. He observed that each description of reality become self-referent, and, to arrive at knowledge, we have to start by knowing ourselves as we relate to the world. This means that, in order to make inquiries into inter-personal relationships, the observer enters into the reality he is observing with his whole self; the quality of the information he gathers therefore depends, above all, on the nature of the relationship established between himself and the person being observed. The job of the therapist is to observe the way in which individuals perceive, explain, interpret and attribute meaning and intention to the inter-personal relationships they are involved in. The therapeutic relationship thus becomes a process of knowledge and growth in which both sides actively participate, to create a new narrative of family events and relational meaning. Finally, we should point out that, with this lens, the therapist can also decide to work with the individual, as this would not interfere with his ability to keep a focus on the wider relational system that also includes him. In other words, it is possible to speak of a client system, referring by this term to the whole family, to a subsystem (for example, that of siblings) or to a single member.

Stern, a psychiatrist and psychoanalyst, has been able, with his studies on *implicit knowledge and inter-subjective consciousness*, to integrate psychoanalytic ideas and systems theories, bridging the gap that separated them. He was not even a family therapist! Some of his statements are very challenging, such as when he states that action is the main road to knowledge or that implicit knowledge is of vital importance in psychotherapy, thus confronting the Freudian method to "make the unconscious conscious". The field of implicit relational knowledge is non-verbal, non-symbolic, unspoken and unconscious. It consists of movements, affective patterns, expectations and even cognitive schemes. Most of what we know about our relationship with others, including transference, forms part of this implicit relational knowledge (Stern, 2004). The concept of implicit knowledge is a legacy of systemic-relational therapies based on experience, like the one practised by myself for over 40 years. The concept of inter-subjective consciousness and the rewriting of the past in the present, as formulated by Stern, have extraordinary implications and offer a confirmation of what we have long stated intuitively, that in family therapy is *the story that heals*.

References

Ackerman, N. W. (1958). *The Psychodynamics of Family Life*. New York: Basic Books.

Anderson, H. & Goolishian, H. A. (1988). Human Systems as Linguistic Systems: Preliminary and Evolving Ideas about the Implications for Clinical Theory. *Family Process*, 27(4), 3–12.

Andolfi, M. (Ed.) (2002). *I Pionieri della Terapia Familiare*. Milan: Franco Angeli.

Andolfi, M. & Angelo, C. (1988). Toward Constructing the Therapeutic System. *Journal of Marital and Family Therapy*, 14, 237–247.

Andolfi, M. & Mascellani, A. (2013). *Teen Voices: Tales of Family Therapy* .San Diego: Wisdom Moon Publishing.

Bateson, G. (1979). *Mind and Nature: A Necessary Unity*. New York: Dutton.

Bateson, G., Jackson, D. D., Haley, J. & Weakland, J. (1956). Toward a theory of schizophrenia. *Systems Research and Behavioral Sciences*, 1(4), 251–264.

Berger, M. (Ed.) (1978). *Beyond the Double Bind. Communication and Family Systems Theories and Techniques with Schizophrenics*. New York: Brunner/Mazel.

Bocchi, G. & Ceruti, M. (Eds.) (1985). *La Sfida della Complessità*. Milan: Feltrinelli.

Boszormenyi-Nagy, I. & Framo J. L. (Eds.) (1965). *Intensive Family Therapy*. New York: Hoeber.

Boszormenyi-Nagy, I. & Spark, G. (1973). *Invisible Loyalties: Reciprocity in Intergenerational Therapy*. New York: Harper & Row.

Bowen, M. (1978). *Family Therapy in Clinical Practice*. New York: Jason Aronson.

Capra, F. (1982). *The Turning Point, Science, Society and the Rising Culture*. New York: Simon and Schuster.

Ceruti, M. (1994). *Constraints and Possibilities: The Evolution of Knowledge and Knowledge of Evolution*. New York: Gordon & Branch.

Framo, J. L. (1992). *Family of Origin. An Intergenerational Approach*. New York: Routledge.

Framo, J. L., Weber, T. & Levine, F. B. (2003). *Coming Back Again: A Family of Origin Consultation*. New York: Routledge.

Haley, J. (1969). An Editorial Farewell. *Family Process*, 8(2), 149–158.

Haley, J. (1976). *Problem-Solving Therapy*. San Francisco: Jossey-Bass.

Haley, J. & Hoffman, L. (1981). *Foundation of Family Therapy*. New York: Basic Books.

International conference on *The Pioneers of Family Therapy*. Rome: Accademia di Psicoterapia della Famiglia, 8–10 December 2000.

Mc Namee, S. & Gergen, K. J. (Eds.) (1992). *Therapy as a Social Construction*. London: Sage.

Miller, J. G. (1978). *Living Systems*. New York: McGraw-Hill.

Minuchin, S. (1972). Structural Family Therapy. In P. J. Kaplan (Ed.) *American Handbook of Psychiatry*. New York: Basic Books, pp. 178–192.

Minuchin, S. (1974). *Families and Family Therapy*. Cambridge, MA: Harvard University Press.

Minuchin, S. (2002). Una Coperta di Pezze per la Terapia Familiare. In M. Andolfi (Ed.). *I Pionieri della Terapia Familiare*. Milan: Franco Angeli.

Selvini Palazzoli, M., Boscolo, L., Cecchin, G. & Prata G. (1978). *Paradox and Counter-paradox: A New Model in the Therapy of the Family in Schizophrenic Transaction*. New York: Jason Aronson.

Selvini Palazzoli, M., Boscolo, L., Cecchin, G. & Prata G. (1980). Hypothesizing, Circularity, Neutrality: Three Guidelines for the Conduction of the Session. *Family Process*, 19(1), 3–12.

Stern, D. N. (2004). *The Present Moment in Psychotherapy and Everyday Life*. New York: Norton.

Telfener, U. (2002). Le Mille Vite di J. Haley: Un Percorso Polifonico. In M. Andolfi (Ed.) *I Pionieri della Terapia Familiare*. Milan: Franco Angeli, pp. 103–114.

Ugazio, V. (1985). Oltre la Scatola Nera. *Terapia Familiare*, 19, 73–83.

Von Bertalanffy, L. (1968). *General Systems Theory*. New York: Braziller.

Von Foerster, H. (1981). *Observing Systems*. Seaside, CA: Intersystems Publications.

Watzlawick, P., Beavin, J. H. & Jackson, D. D. (1967). *Pragmatics of Human Communication. A Study of Interactional Patterns, Pathologies, and Paradoxes*. New York: Norton.

Whitaker, C. A. (1989). *Midnight Musings of a Family Therapist*. New York: Norton.

2

THE FAMILY LIFE CYCLE AND THE MULTI-GENERATIONAL DIMENSION

Every family presents its own individual and complex temporal architecture characterized by the intersecting of individual histories with shared experiences and inter-generational ties. Time is organized along the evolutionary lines of the past, bound by myths and traditions transmitted by the older generations, and along those of a present life, inspired by the elders' expectations and values and shaped by the younger generation's projects for the future. Therefore, the family has a past, a present and a future life perspective and this represents a distinction from other social groups. A newly constituted couple is, in fact, located at the intersection of two family histories that have their roots in a complex genealogical tree, which influences the development of the newly formed nucleus in a very significant way. The new couple's relationship, in effect, is not just made up of the events experienced together from their choice of partner, courtship and falling in love, and their commitment to live together, but is also formed by the inter-weaving of the histories of the two families of origin. It is not only the traces of this past that are present, but also the lines of a future, even though mostly at an implicit and inner level. The new family thus slips into a very rich temporal flow, punctuated and continually transformed by the timing of births and deaths, by periods of growth, and the entrances and exits of the various members of the family system, following its own specific life cycle.

The family life cycle theory

Several authors have described the family life cycle as a theoretical model that looks at the development of the family as a dynamic process characterized by certain developmental stages which require changes and family reorganization (Haley, 1973; Minuchin, 1974; Carter & McGoldrick, 1980, 1988; Walsh, 1982; Duval & Miller, 1985; Mattessich & Hill, 1987; Andolfi, Angelo & de Nichilo, 1989; Becvar, 2007; Andolfi & Mascellani, 2013). The various stages of the family life cycle are considered universal, marked by specific significant events; births and deaths, separations and unions, inclusions and exclusions of members are normal and expected phenomena in any given family. The authors listed above broadly agree on several main transitional periods: the separation from the family of origin and single young adulthood, the formation of a new couple, the family with young children, the family with adolescent children, children leaving home, the reorganization of the parental couple, the ageing parents' later life, having grandchildren and finally death.

These critical stages in the life span of the family are considered *normative events* according to Carter and McGoldrick (1980, 1988), as they pertain to the natural evolution of the family system. The fact that these events are predictable and expected does not mean that they represent easy transitions, or that the family's coping system functions in the same way for different families, or within different cultures and contexts. For example, events like a child's birth, an adolescent leaving home and the death of an elderly parent can acquire very different meanings, and are characterized by very diverse social and family rituals. Some of these transitions can cause a lot of stress and pain to individual members, as well as to the family, and therapy is frequently requested because of difficulties in transitioning from one stage to the next.

Individual symptoms, especially in children or adolescents, are often a clear signal of the complexity a family faces in coping with stages that require the rearrangement of roles and functions, and especially a shift in the caregiving and the affective dimension. For example, the birth of a first child is an exciting new event for most families, but at the same time it requires a transformation of the loving relationship between two partners in order to include a third person – the baby – into their intimate world. Children leaving home require a rearrangement of the parents' life, as they have to renegotiate their emotional stance, and find a new adjustment and maturity in their couple relationship. In contrast, we also see a growing number of adult children who left home forced to return to their parents' house because of an illness, relational problems or financial setbacks. This event has been creating a *boomerang generation* and a new *crowded-nest syndrome* (Shaputis, 2003; Collins, Jordan & Coleman, 2007). Further transformations are often observed following the death of an elderly parent/grandparent. Each family will handle the issue of an expected but significant loss with very different attitudes. Grief and mourning are not standard emotional responses and families cannot learn from books how to deal with their suffering and get on with their lives. Some families will have access to more resources and skills to deal with periods of developmental crisis. Others will perceive any change as a threat and will struggle. Some will find support within the extended family, their network of friendships and their social system, while others will feel isolated and lonely.

The life cycle model, therefore, allows the therapist to identify the phase that the family is passing through, but also to explore and evaluate family change and reorganization in the transition from one phase to another. The picture becomes more complex if we take into consideration what Carter and McGoldrick (1988) and Walsh (1982) described regarding the stress produced in family transitions, as it is the family as a whole, rather than individual members, that feels the pressure and the burden of multi-generational change. While one generation approaches old age, the next is dealing with the empty-nest syndrome (children leaving home), the third is busy with becoming adult and forming a new couple while the fourth, the birth of a child, begins the process of becoming the new member of the family system. This describes the life cycle of the traditional family, where the couple remains intact, and there is a clear definition in the roles and functions of the parental couple and the children. New types of family will be described in the following chapter; step or blended families, single-parent families, inter-cultural families, migrant families, adoptive families and same-sex families. Although they differ a great deal in terms of composition, roles and functions, they can still be approached using the same systemic-developmental framework.

Several authors, such as Rodgers (1973) and Aldous (1990), criticized the Family Life Cycle Theory, as it was originally described. In particular, they challenged the distinction between *normative* and *para-normative* events. Phenomena like marital separation and divorce, which are now as widespread and statistically relevant as lifelong marriage, cannot be classified as not pertaining to normal family development. Not to mention other dramatic, unexpected and unpredictable family events such as long-lasting illnesses, sudden losses, migration, family disconnections and more. Is there, in reality, a family that does not have to cope with some unexpected and adverse life condition? These authors suggested abandoning the "too deterministic" family life cycle concept in favour of a more dynamic life span-oriented concept, which Rodgers called *the family career*. This book will not enter into an academic debate about this, but will mainly describe families in their multi-generational development, focusing on the main events that have a significant emotional impact on their lives, and on the specific way they confront periods of crisis and transformation.

Multi-generational family narrative

Birth is often described as a leap into the dark, which is a falsehood. The truth is that we are not greeted by emptiness, but by a safety net. Being born is like being thrown into a book already peopled by characters and stories; it is to be exposed to a reality whose rules are already partially written. Our presence will alter the thread of this narrative, perhaps even the ending, but we will never be able to separate ourselves from the pages that precede our entrance, and those pages will inevitably influence us because we are their children. The history of every family is a complex and singular weaving of individual stories, inter-generational ties and shared experiences that follow each other in a time scale delineated not as much by the passage of time as by the succession of one generation by another. Even though, compared to the past, the modern family may be more fragmented, members of the family are still held together by invisible threads, which connect through the passage of time, the past, present and future, and serve to connect a sense of belonging of every generation to a particular family tree. The result is that each individual, though remaining the creator in charge of his/her own individual history, inevitably participates in the acting out of a script that is inter-generational, because each member is born in a certain position in a family. Members are implicitly expected to respond to expectations and roles, and to submit, more or less unconsciously, to those processes that dictate the inter-generational transmission of norms, values and behaviours (Zuk & Boszormenyi-Nagy, 1969; Boszormenyi-Nagy & Spark, 1973; Bowen, 1978; Scabini & Marta, 1995; Andolfi & Mascellani, 2013).

Even the choice of personal or first names for children can be a response to inter-generational expectations and roles, and to cultural norms. Cultural norms may dictate that certain names are given according to birth order or gender that are connected with the names of preceding generations. Names can also be repeated through the generations to honour a deceased family member in order to fill the gap or the loss experienced. This can be a great weight to carry through life. Sometimes, people change their given names because they are trying to escape or get rid of whatever they feel is imbued in the name they were given at birth. Warring parents can sometimes divide children by giving their children names that reflect their side of the family. For example, in one cross-cultural family I met, with an Indian father and English mother, the oldest girl was given a name that was her father's name rearranged, while the second daughter was given a name that was her mother's name rearranged. In this way, each parent claimed a child into their camp that sadly, was reflective of the two divided camps in the family, East vs. West.

In other cases, children can develop symptoms and present for therapy because of the weight of family myths they carry, as in the case of Ciro, a 15-year-old boy who came to therapy for depression. In exploring Ciro's family history, I discovered that Ciro had been born after the death of an older brother, who had been given the name Ciro, in honour of his esteemed belated grandfather who had been a very important figure in the village. The third passing of this personal name created a huge weight for this boy, who had to bear the weight of both a heroic grandfather and the tragic loss of a first-born son.

To observe a family over the span of three generations is to honour the fact that the elders share with the younger generations a cyclical narrative in which individuals have to face universal life events. Each generation undergoes existential changes such as those relating to the birth of a child, the loss of a spouse, the passage from adolescence into adulthood and so on. These evolutionary stages have already been worked through and overcome by the elders in the family, and form the accumulation of experiences that provide additional resources that are transmitted to the newly formed family. From the examples given, we have to ask ourselves how much freedom individuals are allowed to forge their own path, and how the experiences and expectations of preceding generations can be of use.

Invisible loyalties

Taking into account the repetitive nature of certain family events that reappear within the different generations of one family, Boszormenyi-Nagy and Spark (1973) noticed the existence of easily identifiable inter-generational models of relating. The individual, internalizing and obeying the unexpressed rules present in the system, develops a series of loyalties to it that are transmitted from one generation to the next and that are not easily avoided. Each relationship within a family is influenced by loyalty and respect for the multi-generational narrative and its mandates. The adult who provides care and attention to the child becomes, in turn, creditor of a series of "debts" that the child will have to repay. Such existential debts by children to their parents are not easily discharged in a short period, according to Boszormenyi-Nagy and Spark, and shape the foundation of trans-generational connections. Sometimes the "account" between parents and children remains active even when the children become adults and form their own family. In some cases, the account is discharged by the arrival of the third generation, offered as a gift to the first as restitution for what was received. The marital bond represents a decisive step towards individuation from one's family of origin, but, at times, the parents perceive the new ties of loyalty towards the spouse as disloyalty toward them. Therefore, there exist vertical and horizontal loyalties that intersect each other, rendering fundamental the need to balance and make the old and new "duties" compatible, so as not to create conflict between the various levels. The couple is the meeting point between that which has been transmitted to them, and that which, in its turn, they transmit. It is important to note that invisible loyalties do not have to be fulfilled. Rather, they have to be challenged. Goff (2001) and Goldenberg and Goldenberg (2008) provide an overview of the application of Boszormenyi-Nagy's contextual therapy ideas.

The conquest of personal authority

Williamson (1981, 1991), on the other hand, calls this process of individuation and of discharging of inter-generational debts the conquest of personal authority. This is primarily an individual achievement that does not allow for compromises between generations. Only when an adult has reached this intrinsic authoritativeness can she sense her full adulthood and eventually become a parent relying on a good level of self-esteem and self-confidence, no longer depending emotionally on her family of origin. According to Williamson, in order to reach full psychological maturity, autonomy and personal authority are crucial to rebalance the inter-generational dynamics, preventing the older generation licence to reward or punish. The role of parents must undergo a transformation that will force them to descend from a hierarchical level to assume an egalitarian position with their adult child. The role of the adult child must also transform; only by challenging the need to diminishing oneself, so intrinsic in the sense of duty and obligation of paying respect to parents, can one gain more autonomy and freedom. Of course, in this process we cannot underestimate the pressure of cultural traditions and social rules, rooted in many cultures to maintaining a kind of deference/devotion toward older people, often forcing adults into a position of intimidation and submissiveness towards elderly parents. While Boszormenyi-Nagy insists that the invisible loyalties can be discharged only by repaying the debts, Williamson maintains that it is the offspring who can and must initiate the transformation that will end the inter-generational intimidation. This can only happen if the young adult stops fearing freedom, takes up his responsibilities with courage and is ready to let go of the need for parents to guide him in life. This complex process of reaching an "I position" (Bowen, 1978), without emotional dependence on one's parents, is a long one and can only be completed at around 35–40 years of age.

Family myths as an expression and vehicle for family culture

The history of preceding generations transmits meanings and values even when we do not refer to it directly or consciously, but comes to us through our parents' or grandparents' memories, life events, social traditions and rituals, which inform us about past relationships and patterns of communication transmitted to the younger generations over time. Therefore, the cultural identity of a family is comprised of a system of values and beliefs created during the family life cycle, often amplified by the norms and habits of a specific social context and transmitted through generations. This acts to inform and influence how to perform family roles (father, mother and sibling), as well as how to cope with significant life events (deaths, separations, births).

There exists, in fact, a kind of family script that is a reading of events and reality, formed by at least three generations over time and across cultures. Family scripts are a representation of specific family myths, and were described first by Ferreira (1963), and then by several other authors (Byng-Hall, 1979, 1995; Whitaker & Keith, 1981; Falicov, 1983; Seltzer & Seltzer, 1983; Di Nicola, 1985, 1997; Carter & McGoldrick, 1988; Andolfi et al., 1989; Andolfi & Mascellani, 2013). The myth becomes a scheme through which reality is interpreted, and in which real and fantasy elements coexist, inherited in part from the family of origin and partly constructed by the current family. Specific events of family and individual life, especially during critical phases (births, deaths, weddings, marital separations, chronic illness, economic crises, accidents), can arouse strong emotional reactions and huge family tensions, causing each family member to assume a different role and function according to his or her position in that specific mythical constellation. Consequently, a myth becomes a matrix of consciousness (Levi-Strauss, 1981; Lemaire, 1984), representing an element of union between certain family members and a cohesive factor for those who believe in this truth. To create a myth therefore means to translate a series of real events and behaviours into a narrative accepted by all, in which each individual can discover a key to reading his own daily experience and the meaning of his life, while feeling at the same time that he is participating along with the rest of the group. Let us look at an example.

The story of Marco

The example of Marco, a dissolute, unmarried uncle who lived for the moment, with no concern for the value of money and no regrets for his irresponsible actions, can help us to understand better the relationship between a family's myths and culture. The creation of a myth is connected to the amplification, over time, of certain traits and behaviours of someone within a given family and cultural context. Therefore, the mythical figure of Marco, whether considered irresponsible or eccentric, can assume certain absolute attributes for the family members over time. According to this family myth, Marco never regretted anything, was always cheerful and childish in the way he lived his life and displayed an inability to manage money in every situation. This image assumed more grandiose connotations after his death. The memory of Marco, now deceased, was amplified in the little village in which he lived. Marco's irresponsible behaviour was minimized and justified as a reaction to the sudden loss of his father in a car accident when he was a child. Stories that enhanced his notorious character were proverbially remembered, like the time he squandered a large sum of money on gambling, or the story of a woman who remained a spinster for the rest of her life because he betrayed her.

Myths, like fables, are constructed from an interconnected network of events, characters, roles and symbolic contents within which arise certain organizing elements of particular importance in tracing a theme or a plot (Andolfi et al., 1989). This story, originating in Marco's real life, is the product of a collective narrative, based on facts and anecdotes, which resonated throughout the small village and was transmitted to the following generations. But, what is the other side of the family story? In contrast to Marco, his sister was instead remembered as the self-sacrificing woman who was over-responsible, the first-born child who took care and played a parental role with her siblings, within a very poor, fatherless family. Later, she married a man who was the carbon copy of Marco, with the same immature and unfaithful behaviour. Maria spent all her life caring for others, trying to compensate firstly for Marco's shortcomings, and later for her husband's ones, sending a clear message to her children that you cannot expect anything good from men! In fact, for the next two generations all the women in this family were over-responsible and sacrificed themselves for the sake of the family, while the majority of men had problems in school, were later unemployed and became involved in petty crime. Every family member had a role to play in a very complementary family drama, reinforced by the "village moral codes", which did not allow for separation from or betrayal of the community's expectations, where it was "normal" that the women should be the servants of men.

The following paragraphs will discuss how to escape from rigid roles and become free of very damaging family myths, such as the one just described. The collective ownership of myths, besides facilitating the continuity of certain cultural traditions through time, strongly contributes to the strengthening of ideological-affective inter-dependence among family members. Sharing a myth, for the individual, means reinforcing the sense of belonging that ensures the individual a distinct position within a protective niche, and, for the family, a cultural identity that is easily relatable. However, for this to happen and for the myth to become a resource in the growth of the individual and the family, its elements must not be too rigid or operate as prescriptive devices. In fact, it is often the case that, during periods of transition in the family life cycle, the myths themselves come under attack from one or more family member, who signals discomfort regarding a way of belonging that is no longer satisfactory. Sometimes the emergence of individual psychopathology can be a strong message asking for the transformation and evolution of rigid family myths. For example, in the story of Marco and his family, a woman in one of the following generations, tired of being a "slave" to the men, might develop a deep depression or might become an alcoholic or a man might end up in prison or suffer a psychotic breakdown. These symptoms are all messages that speak of a need to change stereotyped roles and functions within the family. Being unconsciously bound to unhealthy family myths can cause a lot of suffering and pain and exact too high a price for survival, and need to be dissolved in therapy in order to bring about new and different dynamics in the family relationships and functions.

The truth at dinner with sons and daughters

A family had been living life under the narrative umbrella of a very special father who died too young, but who had been a heroic figure dedicated to the family, a very hard worker who supported a large family of nine children. He had died when the children were still young, and the mother, for the sake of the children, kept his memory alive by building the image of this special human being. As in the case of Marco, the female children in this family were very responsible, while the males, in contrast, tended to be overly dependent and immature, and displayed problems at work and violent misconduct in the neighborhood. This family went for therapy when the youngest boy, aged 20, started to abuse drugs and developed a borderline personality. Through therapy with this family, the mother finally revealed the truth. She invited all her grown-up children to her house and in tears she admitted that their father was not the "hero" that she had invented for them. On the contrary, from the very beginning of their marriage, he had been a very unreliable man who had gambled and lost a lot of money, while she worked hard to keep the family together and to support the children. The positive outcome of this dramatic and courageous revelation by the mother was immediately evident in the next session through the new expressions on the children's faces. They finally knew the truth about their father, and were more understanding of their mother's lie, kept alive for so long. Instead of getting angry with her for the falsehood she had constructed and imposed on their lives, they felt relieved as they could finally free themselves of the imposed stereotypes – responsible women and failing men. The children were finally able to appreciate the sacrifices and courage of a mother who had brought up nine children single-handedly, attending to all their needs. The debunking of the family myth allowed for freedom from an implicit imposition of stereotyped roles. Each family member gained a new sense of authenticity through the mother's revelation. For her part, she was able to discharge an incredible burden and demonstrate new respect towards herself and her children. The siblings were able to be a new team and support their brother, who improved greatly from that point onwards.

The differentiation of self

Bowen's Family Systems Theory was one of the first comprehensive theories of family development functioning over generations, and has been well described in his pioneering book, *Family Therapy in Clinical Practice* (1978), as well as in several other publications (Andolfi, 1979; Kerr & Bowen, 1988; Papero, 1990; Innes, 1996; Rasheed, Rasheed & Marley, 2011). His theoretical approach had an enormous influence on the family therapy movement in the United States for over 30 years, and his model of multi-generational family functioning, developed at Georgetown University in Washington, DC, is still used in studies and research today, and has been expanded and further investigated in Europe as well as in other parts of the world. According to Bowen, in the span of only 150–200 years, an individual is the descendant of 64–128 families, each of which has contributed something to him. With all the myths, mystifications, loyalties, memories and opinions influenced by our emotional systems, it is often difficult to recognize our own personal self. As no therapist had done before or since, Bowen went far back through generations, to reconstruct the family history and to find in the past clues and connections with the present. His study was centred on the individual and his history, and its aim was to individuate the former from what he called the "ego family mass", which corresponds to a state of total fusion.

Murray Bowen was the eldest of five children of a family belonging to the rural *bourgeoisie* in Tennessee, United States. In 1937, he completed a doctorate in medicine. His experience as a medical officer during the Second World War sparked his interest in psychiatry. At the end of the war, he worked at the Menninger Clinic in Topeka with schizophrenic children and their mothers. In 1954, he transferred to the National Institute of Mental Health, in Washington, where whole families were treated and helped. Bowen's work with the mother–child dyad helped him to realize that dyadic relationships are only two poles of an emotional triangle. Fathers, even when perceived to be absent or emotionally distant, are the third pole that needs to be included in the observation of family dynamics. He described the triangle as the smallest stable relationship (Kerr & Bowen, 1988). "Triangling" (he never used the word triangulation; that became present later in Minuchin's structural approach) occurs when the inevitable anxiety in a dyad is relieved by involving a vulnerable third party who either takes sides or provides a detour for the anxiety (Guerin, Fogarty, Fay & Kautto, 1996).

Bowen's focus was on the patterns that develop in families in order to defuse anxiety. A key generator of anxiety is the perception of either too much emotional closeness or too great a distance in the relationship. From this, he developed the concept of the differentiation of self from the family of origin, the cornerstone of his theory, in which the high level of emotional fusion within the family is the obstacle to a person having a clear perception of him-/herself as a complete self in relation to others. The result of this separation process through a continuous effort of self-definition and individuation would become known as differentiation. However, such a process cannot transpire exclusively at the level of the current relationships between members in the nuclear family or in a couple, but must take place by entering into the respective families of origin, to enable the individual to gain freedom and awareness within a system of relationships that has become open and flexible. Differentiation naturally requires a lifelong effort on the part of the individual, and is certainly not exempt from obstacles and blockages. Differentiation is influenced by various factors, such as the degree of emotional stress and anxiety produced in the nuclear family, which in turn is affected by the level of emotional separation/defusion from the family of origin and by the process of maturity/immaturity transmitted through generations. The concept of the family of origin as a resource in couple and family work was born from the conviction of the existence of trans-generational forces that exercise a critical influence on present relationships.

Bowen used the term *coaching* to describe his way of conducting therapy with families in difficulty or to do supervision with his students. In both situations he used to collect elaborate family genograms, and discussed with clients and students a concrete way to "return home". He explained that this was a kind of mission that required much time, and that the effort it took allowed people to become better observers, and that learning more about the family reduces emotional reactivity, which, in turn, helps them to become better observers (Bowen, 1978). Going back home not only has a reconciliatory effect between one generation and the next; it also allows the person to experience her most significant relationships with a different and more mature awareness of her own self (Andolfi, 2002). Through the construction of a scale of differentiation, Bowen placed the various levels of emotional involvement within the family along a continuum, from extreme fusion to total differentiation of the self. At the lowest range of the scale, we find those individuals who function in a substantially fused position to the Ego Family Mass and who during their life will look for very dependent connections from which they derive the strength necessary to function. Complete emotional maturity corresponds to a total differentiation of the self. The people belonging to this category represent the highest levels of emotional functioning and their capacity to establish differentiated but emotionally qualifying relationships with their own family of origin that also benefit the nuclear family. It is rare to come across such highly differentiated individuals either in therapy or in social encounters.

Emotional cut-off

The search for balance between belonging and separation is a difficult process that follows an individual throughout life and that, unfortunately, is not always successful. We often remain trapped in unsatisfactory, compulsively repeated relational models. Belonging and separation represent two emotional positions, both necessary to the goal of differentiation; they are two peaks of the wave motion characteristic of the emotional dynamics specific to harmonious affective relationships, from parent–child to couple. Not infrequently, however, instead of being perceived as phases, they are experienced as mutually exclusive concepts: if we belong, separation is not possible; if we separate, we must renounce belonging. If fusion is defined as the belonging that does not tolerate separation, emotional cut-off represents the opposite, equally problematic, extreme: a person's sudden, often conflictual, physical and/or emotional distancing from familial and emotional ties (Bowen, 1978). It is a condition of profound estrangement by one or more members of a family that "protects" from confrontation on "unfinished business" and from experiencing feelings of disconnection from very important family and cultural bonds. Such relational modality, a cardinal concept in Relational Psychology, can produce evolutionary impasses and feelings of emotional incompleteness in adulthood that will produce discomfort and malaise not only in the individual, but also in the couple and parent–child relationship. It is often caused by the illusion that independence can be gained just by leaving home and refusing all contact with the family of origin. On the contrary, the unresolved issues with the family of origin will weigh even more heavily on the fugitive, repeating themselves unconsciously in other relationships and forcing the individual to seek compensatory ties to fill the "void" and anaesthetize the pain.

The condition of partial, or sometimes total, cut-off from family and social roots nowadays is even more dramatic because of the increasing number of migrating families in many parts of the world, which often produces an existential disquiet that permeates both the parental relationship and friendships. This compelled a number of pioneer therapists (Minuchin, Montalvo, Rosman & Schumer, 1967; Andolfi, 1979; Falicov, 1983; Di Nicola, 1985, 1997; Sluzki, 1992; Mollica, 2006) to talk about cultural family therapy, focusing more on the social and cultural components of family ruptures and cut-off. To complete this process of differentiation and reach what Bowen called the "I position" (Bowen, 1978), it is necessary to become an adult and to reconnect and reconcile with the past by working through losses, traumas and open conflicts with extended-family members.

Inter-generational intimidation and the chronic child

The term *chronic child* has been coined to describe an adult who has never been able to assume a mature role in his/her own family, remaining stuck in a child-like position, depending emotionally on parents or partners or sometimes even on an older sibling (Andolfi, 2003; Andolfi, Falcucci, Mascellani, Santona & Sciamplicotti, 2007). Through my clinical experience, I found a series of dysfunctional relational patterns, especially in couple dynamics, where one partner plays the role of the mother/father to the other, who remains emotionally blocked at a younger developmental stage. This immaturity in assuming full responsibility as an adult seems to be directly connected to the inability/impossibility of standing up to parents in the family of origin.

This concept is very close to what Williamson (1981, 1991), described as "inter-generational intimidation", which arrests the process of acquiring the personal authority necessary for the individual to reach full psychological maturity. He conceptualized the existence of a specific stage in the family life cycle, the fundamental purpose of which consists in overcoming the hierarchical limits in the parent–adult child relationship by establishing a more egalitarian position. Often, life events and the construction of family myths around this issue condition the process of emotional growth for individuals, who can become very competent and respected professionals in the social arena, but remain as dependent children in front of their parents and families. In spite of the fact that the dependence is reciprocal, it is the adult child who must transform this dynamic through an authentic and active move, which the older generation will, in time, come to acknowledge and respect. An eventual break in the dependency by a parent is likely to be experienced as abandonment, whilst a renegotiation of power by the younger person leads to authentic maturity and becomes proof of that person outgrowing the child position. Maturity actually consists in no longer needing a parent (Williamson, 1981; Lawson, 2011). The parent who witnesses such maturity in the child will spontaneously start to develop a different kind of relationship, a more intimate and egalitarian one.

Establishing a relationship of reciprocity with parents allows grown children to appreciate better their parent's humanity and to get to know the individual behind the parental roles. This primary experience creates equality between generations and dissolves inter-generational intimidation (Bray, Williamson & Malone, 1986). Reaching such a goal offers the adult enormous advantages in the relationship within the couple, and in their own parental and professional roles. Many couples reach a point where their relationship deteriorates because they have not been able to defend their space as a couple from intrusion by their respective family of origin. Even though invasion by one or other of the parents can spoil the couple relationship, it is always an excessive dependence by the adult and his/her inability to separate effectively from the family of origin which facilitates the intrusion. It is, therefore, the children who must finally choose the role their parents play in relation to their life plan, how and why to involve them, how much they still need to remain children and whether they can risk taking on new roles and challenges.

Graduating as an adult son

Giovanni and Laura, a middle-aged married couple, requested therapy at the point when they were very close to separation because of the constant requests for help and assistance from Giovanni's old mother, from whom the son seemed unable to separate emotionally. In order to understand the current problems facing the couple, it was necessary to explore Giovanni's early years. Giovanni had grown up in a small village in Italy, which after the Second World War underwent a great process of migration. Giovanni's father went to work in the mines in Belgium, working hard to send money back to his young wife and son. Little Giovanni grew up as an only child, with a very demanding mother and an absent but very important father, respected and idealized because of the sacrifice he made for them. Because of the money his father sent home, Giovanni was able to go to school and finally he became a doctor of medicine. For many years, the "real couple" in the family was made up of mother and child, and they developed a system of mutual loyalties and very collusive bonds, which was never renegotiated even after Giovanni left home, went to live in a big city and married Laura, who was also a busy and respected professional. Giovanni's mother, Maria, was never able to release her son emotionally. Giovanni remained her young son forever and she would request his intervention as a doctor for any minor health problem. Giovanni lived two hours' distance from his mother and was always "on call" for any slight fever, headache and arrhythmia. He was a servant to his mother's ailments and would always run to her aid.

His wife had grown sick and tired of this situation and gave her husband, who was unable to say no to his mother, an ultimatum, threatening to leave him. They came to therapy as a couple in deep crisis and several months were spent working with them before a special meeting was proposed, to which Maria was also invited. During that session, Giovanni finally found the courage to tell his mother that he had always loved and respected her and that she was very important in his life, but that now he wanted his life back and he wanted to take care of himself and of his marriage, which was at the point of collapse. He ended this painful and liberating communication to his mother by saying that from now on he would no longer continue to assist her as a doctor because she had her own general practitioner in the village and his presence was not necessary. This was his declaration of maturity, a sort of "graduation as an adult son" and, surprisingly, the mother, who had been looking in his eyes all the time he spoke, felt her son's pain and care at this special moment of intimacy and embraced him with great affection. This was the very first time, since starting therapy, that Laura was able to respect Giovanni as her husband because of the personal risk he had taken and because he had sent her an implicit message of marital reconciliation.

References

Aldous, J. (1990) Family Development and the Life Course: Two Perspectives on Family Change. *Journal of Marriage and Family Therapy,* 52(3), 571–583.

Andolfi, M. (1979). *Family Therapy – An Interactional Approach.* New York: Plenum Press.

Andolfi, M. (Ed.) (2002). *I Pionieri della Terapia Familiare.* Milan: Franco Angeli.

Andolfi, M. (2003). *Manuale di Psicologia Relazionale.* Rome: A.P.F.

Andolfi, M. & Mascellani, A. (2013). *Teen Voices. Tales of Family Therapy,* San Diego: Wisdom Moon Publishing.

Andolfi, M., Angelo, C. & de Nichilo, M. (1989). *The Myth of Atlas: Families and the Therapeutic Story.* New York: Brunner/Mazel.

Andolfi, M., Falcucci, M., Mascellani, A., Santona, A. & Sciamplicotti, F. (Eds.) (2007). *Il Bambino come Risorsa nella Terapia Familiare.* Rome: A.P.F.

Becvar, D. S. (2007) *Families that Flourish.* New York: Norton.

Boszormenyi-Nagy, I. & Spark, G. (1973). *Invisible Loyalties; Reciprocity in Intergenerational Family Therapy*. New York: Harper & Row.

Bowen, M. (1978). *Family Therapy in Clinical Practice*. New York: Jason Aronson.

Bray, J. H., Williamson, D. S. & Malone, P. E. (1986). An Evaluation of an Intergenerational Consultation Process to Increase Personal Authority in the Family System. *Family Process*, 25(3), 423–436.

Byng-Hall, J. (1979). Re-editing Family Mythology During Family Therapy. *Journal of Family Therapy*, 1(2), 103–116.

Byng-Hall, J. (1995). *Rewriting Family Scripts: Improvisation and System Change*. New York: Guilford Press.

Carter, E. A. & McGoldrick, M. (1980). *The Family Life Cycle: A Framework for Family Therapy*. New York: Gardner Press.

Carter, E. A. & McGoldrick, M. (1988). *The Changing Family Life Cycle: A Framework for Family Therapy* (2nd ed.). New York: Gardner Press.

Collins, D., Jordan, C. & Coleman, H. (2007). *An Introduction to Family Social Work*. Belmont, CA: Brooke & Cole.

Di Nicola, V. F. (1985). An Overview: Family Therapy and Transcultural Psychiatry: An Emerging Synthesis in the Conceptual Basis. *Transcultural Psychiatric Research Review*, 22(2), 81–113.

Di Nicola, V. F. (1997). *A Stranger in the Family: Culture, Families, Therapy*. New York: Norton.

Duval, E. & Miller, B. (1985). *Marriage and Family Development*. New York: Harper & Row.

Falicov, C. J. (1983). *Cultural Perspectives in Family Therapy*. Rockville, MD: Aspen Corporation.

Ferreira, A. J. (1963). Family Myth and Homeostasis. *Archives of General Psychiatry*, 9, 457–463.

Goff, J. K. (2001). Fundamentals of Theory and Practice: Revisited Boszormenyi-Nagy and Contextual Therapy. An Overview. *Australian & New Zealand Journal of Family Therapy*, 22, 147–157.

Goldenberg, H. & Goldenberg, I. (2008). *Family Therapy. An Overview*. Belmont, CA: Brooks & Cole.

Guerin, P. J., Fogarty, T. F., Fay, L. F. & Kautto, J. G. (1996). *Working with Relationship Triangles*. New York: Guilford Press.

Haley, J. (1973). *Uncommon Therapy: the Psychiatric Technique of Milton Erickson*. New York: Norton.

Innes, M. (1996). Connecting Bowen Theory with its Human Origin. *Family Process*, 35, 487–500.

Kerr, M. & Bowen, M. (1988). *Family Evaluation. An Approach Based on Bowen Theory*. New York: Norton,

Lawson, D. M. (2011). Integrated Intergenerational Therapy with Couples. In D. Carson & M. Casado-Kehoe (Eds.) *Case Studies in Couples Therapy*. New York: Routledge, pp. 79–91.

Lemaire, J. G. (1984). "La Réalité Informe, Le Mythe Structure. *Dialogue*, 2, 3–23.

Levi-Strauss, C. (1981). *The Naked Man*. New York: Harper & Row.

Mattessich, P. & Hill, R. (1987). Life Cycle and Family Development. In M. B. Sussman and S. K. Steinmetz (Eds.) *Handbook of Marriage and the Family*. New York: Plenum Press, pp. 437–469.

Minuchin, S. (1974). *Families and Family Therapy*. Cambridge, MA: Harvard University Press.

Minuchin, S., Montalvo, B., Rosman, B. & Schumer, F. (1967). *Families of the Slum*. New York: Basic Books.

Mollica, R. (2006). *Healing Invisible Wounds*. San Diego: Harcourt.

Papero, V. D. (1990). *Bowen System Theory*. London: Pearson.

Rasheed, J., Rasheed M. & Marley, J. (2011). *Family Therapy: Models and Techniques*. London: Sage.

Rodgers, R. (1973). *Family Interaction and Transaction: The Developmental Approach*. Englewood Cliffs, NJ: Prentice-Hall.

Scabini, E. & Marta, E. (1995). *La Famiglia con Adolescenti: uno Snodo Critico Inter-generazionale. Quarto rapporto CISF sulla Famiglia in Italia*. San Paolo: Cinisello Balsamo.

Seltzer, W. J. & Seltzer, M. R. (1983). Material, Myth, Magic: A Cultural Approach to Family Therapy. *Family Process*, 22(1), 3–14.

Shaputis, K. (2003). *The Crowded Nest Syndrome: Surviving the Return of Adult Children*. Centralia, WA: Gorham.

Sluzki, C. (1992). Transformations: A Blueprint for Narrative Changes in Therapy. *Family Process*, 31(3), 217–230.

Walsh, F. (Ed.) (1982). *Normal Family Processes*. New York: Guilford Press.

Whitaker, C. & Keith, D. (1981). Symbolic Experiential Family Therapy. In A. S. Gurman & D. P. Kniskern (Eds.) *Handbook of Family Therapy*. New York: Brunner/Mazel, pp. 187–225.

Williamson, D. S. (1981). Personal Authority via Termination of the Intergenerational Hierarchical Boundary: A New Stage in the Family Life Cycle. *Journal of Marital and Family Therapy*, 7(4), 441–452.

Williamson, D. S. (1991). *The Intimacy Paradox*. New York: Guilford Press.

Zuk, G. B. & Boszormenyi-Nagy, I. (1969). *Family Therapy and Disturbed Families*. Palo Alto, CA: Science Behavior Books.

3

SOCIAL TRANSFORMATION AND NEW FAMILY FORMS

The history of humanity presents an inexhaustible repertoire of ways of organizing and attributing meaning to reproduction and to sexuality, to the alliance between groups and individuals, and therefore, an infinite variety of ways of building families. Sociological, demographic and psychological studies and research have clearly identified the range of family models that have always characterized human societies, highlighting how the family assumes different functions and structures, supporting and nurturing itself through different economic systems. The transition from the patriarchal family of the rural world, extended and economically self-sufficient, to that of the nuclear family of the industrial era is a significant example of this variability. Over the past 50 years, the family has undergone a process of radical transformation in its structure, demographic configuration, and internal and social roles, to assume gradually greater complexity and differences, and even more dramatic fragmentation, to such an extent that today it is impossible to refer to the family as a standard unit. We are faced, instead, with a multiplicity of family configurations characterized by increasing complexity and progressive fragmentation, described by Golombok (2015) as *modern families*. But, in spite of the current family's increased fragility, uncertainty and instability, it still remains founded on strong inter-generational bonds (which, because of today's increased longevity, can extend over four generations), where values, long-term love, caring and goods are shared, and children's growth enabled.

Families and their organization may vary a great deal according to the prevalence of the dominant dyad. In pre-industrial societies, as well as in cultures characterized by strong family traditions as in Eastern societies, the focus was on the parent–child relationship, while in most economically advanced countries there has been a shift on to the couple as the central unit of the family. Parents with double careers and a more egalitarian partner relationship have replaced the older, rigid and hierarchical model of the authoritarian man and housekeeping woman, where the economic and social power imbalance affected the quality of family life. The previous chapter described the life cycle of "traditional" families. This chapter will focus on other family configurations and describe their main traits and relational qualities. Despite differences in family forms, the same multi-generational framework and systemic-developmental approach remain applicable in the understanding and treatment of families.

Children of divorced and single-parent families

In reality, single-parent families are not a new phenomenon. Single-parenthood has been historically common due to high parental mortality rates because of death and wars and as a result of having children outside of wedlock, while in today's reality, single-parent families seem to be much more frequently the result of an increased divorce rate. A single parent is usually considered the primary caregiver, the parent with whom the children reside for most of the time. Universally, mothers have been typically invested with the role of primary caregivers, even though this scenario has shifted in recent years, with many fathers taking an active role as "stay-at-home dads", and more mothers returning to the workforce. In addition, the practice of joint custody has resulted in fathers bonding with and connecting more to their children (McLanahan & Carlson, 2004; Ahrons, 2007).

A mother as a single parent will be more at risk, especially in disadvantaged socio-economic contexts, because of her underprivileged position in the labour market and the overwhelming responsibilities of raising children alone, often with no economic or emotional support from unemployed or absent fathers (Amato, 2000). The number of children from divorced parents is becoming so significant that in the near future it will probably equal that of children of intact couples. Because of the magnitude of this phenomenon (there is an immense body of literature on this subject), we cannot underestimate the damage produced in children by the loss of family unity and harmony that, ideally, is the best condition for healthy and happy growth. Fortunately, children are very resilient and capable of looking for love and care even in very critical situations. Children never welcome the separation of parents, but things are much worse for them when there is a high level of hostility. They can be triangulated, or split, by parents who are unable to deal with their unresolved marital conflicts.

In a single-parent family, it is also very possible that a child will be elevated to a supportive adult role by a parent who is still very wounded or sad because of marital separation. We often underestimate the protection and care provided by children, even at a very young age, towards parents, especially when they feel their pain and loneliness. In this sense, and to a certain degree, the assumption of a parental role in children with single parents is useful, but it might become very damaging to the child if it becomes a long-term necessary function leading to a *role reversal* (Blau, 1993; Whiteman, 1993; Andolfi & Mascellani, 2013). Counselling and psychotherapy can activate positive resources and support from the parents' extended family; an older family member, with more mature experience, might be of help, liberating the "parental child" from the need to take care of the parent in question. In this case, a therapeutic intervention might be requested because of the emergence of psychosomatic, relational or behavioural symptoms in their children, or because of a depressive condition or anxiety in one or other parent. The symptoms can be considered important indicators of relational discomfort and guide therapists into the family's open wounds, such as still-active hostile separation, the absence of one or other parent from the life of the children, or sibling rivalry and competition.

Often, therapists forget to include the person who is no longer living in the house, ignoring the importance of reconnecting the absent/distant parent. Of course, if the couple are divorced it would not be appropriate to work with the entire family as if they were still living together. In these cases, the therapist would see the single parent with the child/children, but will also alternate sessions with the other parent and children, and sometimes see the children by themselves. The idea that it is not important to invite the parent who is not in charge or who does not have custody is a "non-systemic way" of looking at families. Even fathers who have been neglecting their children for a long time should be given the chance to reconnect and learn how to care for their kids (Aquilino, 2006). By enlarging the framework, children triangulated into parents' conflicts can be helped to stop taking sides and to recreate sibling bonds. At the end of this parallel process a joint meeting with parents and children can be proposed to evaluate the progress achieved, including symptom improvement, and to compliment everyone for the great job they have done together (Andolfi & Mascellani, 2013).

Step-parenting and blended families

With the increase in marital separation and divorce all over the world, the creation of blended families is becoming almost equal in number to that of conventional families. However, the process of living together and forming a new, blended family that includes children from one or both partners' previous relationships, often with the addition of their own new children, rarely progresses smoothly. It is a very challenging experience, as described by a number of authors (Visher & Visher, 1991; Bray & Kelly, 1998; Nelsen, Erwin & Glenn, 1997; Steward, 2005; Goldscheider & Sassler, 2006; Michaels, 2006; Greeff & Toit, 2009; King, 2009; Papernow, 2009; Lambert, 2010). Let us consider some of the main issues blended families have to contend with in order to create a solid foundation and live together successfully.

The need to finalize the separation/divorce

Both partners need to have emotionally and financially finalized their previous marriage and survived a painful separation without carrying any unfinished business into their new love relationship. Children of the previous marriages must be able to work through and accept the family separation, with all its consequences, without being rushed into a new family dimension. It is important for children to feel that the marital separation was fair and not fall into the pattern of "winners and losers". Children have a great sense of systemic justice and cannot tolerate unfair endings, or heavy triangulations, which result in taking sides and splitting their sibling alliance. In the case of the death of a parent, the remarriage of the remaining parent may trigger unprocessed grief in children, who need space and time to grieve without being forced to rush and accept the new life configuration.

Preferential loyalty and sibling rivalry

When two adults marry for the first time, they are free to make their own decisions. When they decide to remarry, they must have permission from their children. In fact, parents know well that without their children's agreement and positive attitude toward the new partner, their new life might become a nightmare. Often, remarried mothers are very careful and protective of their children and do not allow their new partner to discipline or give them direct rules, at least in the initial years of their relationship. Their loyalty towards their own children might create favouritism or, at the other extreme, they might overcompensate in the care and attention towards their step-children. Enlarging the sibling community is potentially very enriching, but sometimes jealousy and rivalry for more attention and love might occur, especially when the new couple have their own children, who might also be privileged because of their younger age.

Keeping all parents involved

Children will adjust much better to the blended family if they have access to both biological parents. Therefore, it is very important for all parents to be involved and work toward a parenting partnership. Boys will often have difficulty in accepting a new father figure in blended families, especially if they have spent a long time in a one-parent family lacking the presence of their biological father, but also harbouring the hope of their parents reconciling. They might wish to get their real father back rather than have to accept the newcomer, who has to be careful not to invade a child's delicate emotional space and to adapt to the child's pace. Every child is different, and will show adults how quickly or slowly he needs to connect. Shy, introverted children might require the adult to slow down and give them more time to warm up to them and get their trust.

Maintaining the marriage bond in blended families

There is no doubt that a lot of energy is needed to help children adjust, create boundaries and share parenting responsibilities, but it is essential to build a strong marital bond based on mutual love and care. This will ultimately benefit everyone, including the children. If they see love, respect and open communication between spouses, they will feel more secure and even learn to model those relational qualities.

Single-person families

A further manifestation of the changing aspects of family organization and fragmentation is represented by the increasing number of single-person families, namely of people who live alone. Young people can live alone for a period, but adults may choose this as a lifestyle. They might have a lot of friends and emotional relationships, but with no commitment to share daily life and live under the same roof. In other cases, the choice to remain single could rather be the result of difficulties in forming stable, intimate relationships or may signal a very deep feeling of loneliness and isolation. Adults who have been married and later divorced can live alone for a period, not out of choice but because they fear failing again in a new couple experience. In this sense, women tend to remain single longer, while men seem to be eager to rebuild marital ties more quickly. In our clinical experience, it is not rare to observe that when men re-enter a new couple relationship too quickly, their adolescent children might protest or sabotage the father's new relationship, seeing it as a betrayal toward their mother or themselves. Older people who have lost their partner and live alone form another category of single-person families. There can be a tendency to live more in their memories of many years of marriage and shared life experiences than to live in the present. In other cases, they may be in denial about the loss by making believe that their beloved partner is still there and that nothing has changed in their life. Describing these situations as single-person families is the best way to outline that they are real families, meaning that the multi-generational configuration of their families is still there and alive with affective connections to the older generation (family of origin), and the younger one (children, grandchildren). Therefore being *single* should be considered as a dynamic family dimension, and when therapists are requested to intervene in cases of anxiety, depression, loneliness, sadness, psychosomatic symptoms and even mental disorders suffered by individuals who live alone, to know that the best way to treat this is to activate the extended family resources. Members of the larger family unit can be invited to the session in order to reconnect and recreate affective alliances and bonds, as well as to mourn important losses together. If they cannot be physically present, they can be included in the session in a symbolic way, with a series of activities and rituals that will be described later in this book.

De facto relationships and families

A *de facto* relationship is a term used for certain couples, heterosexual or homosexual, who live together without being legally married. *De facto* couples that are parents are generally subject to the same rules as married parents, concerning parental duties and responsibilities. The increasing development of *de facto* couples is indicative of a crisis in the institution of marriage during the last few decades, but absolutely not a crisis in the relationship of couples. The difficulties young people experience in finding work, the high cost of renting and an increased wish to pursue further education may be named as causes and contributing factors in delaying a marriage commitment, but they hardly provide a complete and comprehensive explanation of the phenomenon. The decrease in the number of marriages can be explained by the decision of an increasing number of couples to choose not to institutionalize their union, even when they decide to have children. The failure of a previous marriage can also lead new partners to begin living together while waiting for the dissolution of the previous bond, or it might encourage men and women to cohabit rather than remarry for fear of a new failure (Roussel, 1989). It is also possible that a *de facto* relationship will shift into an official marriage when children arrive, mainly because of the expectations of the extended family or to ensure better legal protection for the new generation. Ultimately, we have to admit that it is still difficult to find "the reason" for such a choice, especially in heterosexual couples, without taking into consideration radical social transformations, changed lifestyles and personal priorities. Different parameters apply to same-sex couples that, in many parts of the world, are not legally allowed to marry. These issues will be explored later in this chapter.

Adoptive families

"We want a baby so that we can hold him in our arms and also, if he is little, he will not remember his past".

"He let us down, he does not recognize what we did for him, we cannot keep him, and he has caused a crisis between us".

"We have given a lot of thought to our request to adopt a child; we feel we can be good parents; there will be difficulties, but we will manage".

"When I grow up, I will go back to my country and take a lot of presents to everyone".

"My adoptive parents gave a man something. Maybe they sold me".

"Maybe my mother is no longer in Santiago de Chile; the police kept her away so she could not find me. She must be suffering because of this. They keep her away from me".

These short, moving and contradicting sentences capture some of the dilemmas of adoptive parents and express the fears of children who have experienced abandonment, to start a new life, often in another part of the world. The adoption of children has been an increasing phenomenon caused by the increase in infertility rates in the most industrialized countries. The adoptive family presents certain peculiarities that distinguish it from other family types.

Ideally, the arrival of a natural child in a family represents the achievement of a shared desire between the two parents and their own extended kin. For adopting parents and their adopted child, the journey is much more complex. Both parents and child experience a deep sense of loss. The couple often experiences a sense of failure due to their inability to have biological children, often deepened because of a further failure in being unsuccessful in their efforts to have a baby through *in vitro* fertilization. For the child, the new journey starts after the painful experience of being neglected, or abandoned by the biological parents, which is often accompanied by an uprooting from the child's cultural context, language and values.

A successful adoptive process is one in which a child feels welcomed, loved and accepted with all the baggage of previous experiences; from the trauma of abandonment to memories of life events and relationships to significant adults (formed during experiences at foster families, children's home, institutions or hospital facilities), as well as to siblings and peer group. The new parents, on the other hand, feel happy and delighted that after a long period of suffering and disappointment, their dream of having a child has finally been fulfilled. Of course, the success of the adoption is dependent on several important elements. Firstly, the shared motivations of the couple in this process; couples are not always both ready and willing to adopt and to start a new life as a family. Secondly, the level of harmony and mutual support by both partners in creating a positive context for the child, by avoiding involving the "newcomer" in damaging marital conflicts. More essentially, the partners should have worked through the loss of their biological child, and all their sense of previous failures in their attempt to get their own child. Otherwise, there is a possible risk for the adopted child of being forced to fill the emotional void in the parents' life without the freedom to grow as an autonomous person.

The adopted child is not the only one who needs to adapt to the new parents. S/he enters into a new family where extended members have to learn how to adapt their roles and relational patterns caused by his/her arrival, as their support and care are very important for the wellbeing of the child. The family's experience of the adoption can depend on a number of factors, such as the story of the child's origin and early experiences of institutionalization, the issue around the couple's lack of fertility, and the first encounters (the "honeymoon phase") of the parents with the adoptive child (Jewett, 1978; Brodzinsky & Schechter, 1993; Van Guiden & Bartels-Rabb, 1993; D'Andrea, 2001; Sykes, 2001; Brodzinsky & Palacio, 2005; Chistolini, 2010; Andolfi & Mascellani, 2013). The adolescent stage represents a testimony of how successful the adoption process has been. Many issues from the process will re-emerge in adolescence: from the early period of abandonment, to the authenticity of the adoptive parents' motivation and caregiving, and the social success of children in adapting to the extended family, school and peer groups.

A carnival of disasters

Too often in therapy, we see families who are worried and confused about their adopted child's violent behaviour towards one or both parents, or towards a sibling, which is unexpected and often in contrast to their calmer childhood behaviour. Once, during a session, a mother uncovered her long-sleeved shirt to show the large haematoma she had along both her arms: her 12-year-old daughter had bitten her very badly many times, apparently without reason. In working with this family, I learned that the parents went from France to Brazil to adopt two young girls, in much the same manner as if they went there to "buy a new car", with little respect for the girls' past life experiences. When upset by the children's behaviour at home, the parents would remind them that they had saved their lives, telling them that they were just the result of a Brazilian carnival! (During the carnival, when people lose control, many women get pregnant and a significant number of babies are born and abandoned on the streets.) In France, the two young girls grew up in an affluent home and attended private school. However, the girls never felt really loved or taken into consideration. They were also dragged into an intense and unresolved marital conflict, forced to take sides by one parent against the other and often threatened with being given away if they did not behave. Anger and violent behaviour in adopted adolescents, especially in interracial adoptions, are frequent responses to unspoken conflicts and fears from their past, but they are also a dramatic signal of discomfort and despair in situations, such as the one just described (Simon & Altstein, 2002; Boss, 2006). Adoption without love and care might lead to emotional abuse by parents who lack respect for their fragile children, who become the recipients of their sense of impotence and frustration from previous failures in having babies, in their marriage and so on.

Cross-cultural and immigrant families

Couples forming relationships among people from different racial, ethnic and religious backgrounds have been one of the major consequences of centuries of migration. Cross-cultural couples and their families are part of a growing number of family types that have become more prominent in the modern world.

Mixed couples

Firstly, this section will briefly describe couples where one partner belongs to the country that the other came to live in. It will then focus on the more common phenomenon, where both partners are migrants and start a family in a new land. One of the strengths of this union is the mutual acceptance of diversity: cross-cultural couples live with difference and cultivate difference. Differences exist on many levels: linguistic, cultural, religious, physical, emotional, verbal and non-verbal communication. At first, it is diversity itself, at times amplified by cultural stereotypes, that contributes to the attraction between two people (Andolfi, Mascellani & Santona, 2011). The choice of a partner outside one's country of origin has long been considered as a sign of rejection of the rules and values of one's own cultural group. Doubtlessly, the choice of a partner outside one's country can easily be construed by the family of origin as a kind of betrayal or rejection of one's roots. At some levels, it might be described as a form of emotional disconnection that leads to the making of a choice that is opposed by the parents and the community, in an attempt to individuate from them and reclaim the ability to make autonomous choices.

Therefore, mixed couples often face opposition from the family of origin. This is particularly hard in the case of cultural groups that are closed and profoundly protective of their traditions and values system; for example, the existence of arranged marriages in several countries, even nowadays, whereby the parent chooses a partner for their child. In extreme cases, the family's rejection of a mixed marriage can be total and can lead to a distancing and loss of connection between generations. Volker, Terri and Wetchler (2003), conducted very interesting studies with interracial couples.

The social stereotypes and prejudices around mixed marriages can be the cause of profound distress on both personal and relational levels. The birth of a child can be an opportunity for reconnection with the grandparents, but can also become the cause of further tensions, especially in the parental couple. Cross-cultural parents are required to make more choices in comparison to those that share the same cultural and ethnic background in decisions surrounding care and upbringing of their children. Often, there are disagreements on how to raise children and expectations for their future (Hotvedt, 1997). These problems are magnified if the couple divorces. On the positive side, the children of parents from different cultures are exposed to different things and can learn more (languages, for example), and develop a different sensitivity and openness towards an increasingly multicultural society.

Migrant families

The history of migration is not only the story of migrant people, but it is also the story of the land to which they move and of their impact on that culture. It is necessary to understand the cultures they bring with them from their own countries (Sewell, 1996). The migrant family occupies a particular position: it finds itself placed between the community of origin and that of the new land that welcomes them, and this juxtaposition determines the impact of transformations on the life cycle phases of the family. This family is subject to the need to adapt to the requirements, regulations and way of life of the country that welcomes them, but at the same time, they are strongly connected to their own culture of origin with specific links to language, tradition, religion and other cultural aspects. To achieve a good level of integration it is necessary to develop a combined unity through trial and error that take into account two different worlds. The present life of migrant families is constantly accompanied by emotions and memories connected to the past and by doubt and uncertainty regarding the future (Ciola, 1997).

Bonvicini (1992) acutely described the environment in which migrants find themselves, where nothing feels familiar, not the sounds, nor the colours, nor the voices or the smells, nor the streets, nor the homes or the kitchen or the education.

It is hard to find oneself again when even the weeks, the holidays and the months are different! Therefore the migrant is forever travelling, in a perpetual to and fro, between the here and the elsewhere, the present and the past, the children and the grandparents, trying to tame two phases of a reality. Naturally, the migrant has the right to do well in his new environment, but also has the duty not to forget his family and country of origin. The creative synthesis that the migrant family must attempt to achieve often amounts to a painful conquest, made up of obstacles and critical events. A comparison with family models in their host country can lead migrants to adhere proudly to a strong ethical base of solidarity that, actually, involves not only the family nucleus, but also the extended family and neighbours. Such pride might lead to the idealization of the family unit, especially with regard to the relationship with the elders and with the family history they share, almost as though to emphasize their cultural superiority defensively against that of the host country. Such strong family roots make the meaning of migration a collective achievement rather than purely at an individual level, with the aim of ensuring a better economic situation for the family of origin. From this perspective, the first person to migrate is the bearer of a family mandate, and therefore performs a task for the whole nucleus (Scabini & Regalia, 1993).

The family's experience of migration and the solidarity experienced within the culture of origin seem to have a determining effect on the way migrants relate to their environment. In particular, there is evidence of various adaptive models that guide how people relate to the surrounding culture. An inclusive model is characterized by an attempt to establish very close, almost exclusive relationships with other migrants from the same country of origin, in order to create a relational network with a strong protective function on both individual and social levels. This attempt to reproduce the family ethos of the country of origin highlights the differences with the culture of the host country. In contrast, in the expansive model, cross-cultural solidarity does not exclude but, on the contrary, favours openness towards the surrounding culture, where children and parents participate with curiosity and interest in the relational life that pertains to them, such as the workplace, school, social activities and so on. In any case, the issue of renegotiating family boundaries and bonds on the inter-generational level influences the regulation of distance and closeness with the new country. Thus, the first generation is engaged in mediating the impact of the new country's social environment on their relationship with their children and the bond with the family of origin. The children's education is a crucial aspect insofar as it can favour, on the one hand, the process of integration but at the same time might increase family and external conflicts. The children's absorption of the host culture can represent, in the parents' eyes, a danger of rupture in inter-generational continuity and a loss of family culture. Therefore, the position of the second generation's children is very difficult: they will adapt better and more quickly to the host culture than the first generation, but they may pay a high price for this adaptive success in terms of progressive estrangement from their family and values. In these cases, social integration can be perceived as a betrayal of the loyalty due to the family and the result is a difficulty in fully identifying with and belonging to the culture of origin or the host culture.

It is the task of the third generation of migrants to connect the past to the future, the cultural needs of the family of origin to the social environment of the adopted country. This generation will feel freer to reclaim aspects of their ethnic identity, sacrificed by the previous generations for the purpose of integration into the chosen culture (Carter & McGoldrick, 2005). In theory, the "between" position of the migrant, or of those who belong to a cultural minority, can be considered a further resource, because it can offer more than one choice, in that it can facilitate greater mobility between two cultural alternatives, useful for establishing social relationships in the new country. In reality, this advantageous position only exists when migrants can easily move from one position to the other by taking the best from the two cultures, without experiencing the danger of not being able to return to the original position. Serious difficulties can emerge when migrants are forced to forsake their own culture in order to assimilate to the host culture. Another difficulty arises when migrants remain strongly anchored to their roots with a sense of refusal and closed-mindedness towards the new culture. Several dangerous situations have been found to produce serious existential malaise: the fear of losing one's roots, the invisible loyalties that are set up in every story of uprooting and of emotional disconnection, the illusion of stopping time, the diversity perceived as a threat to one's existence and the desperate defence of one's traditions (Di Nicola, 1997; McGoldrick & Hardy, 2008).

Homosexual couples and children of same-sex parents

Nowadays, same-sex couples are no longer subjected to the same level of social and family prejudice and stigma as in the past, even though today homosexual marriages are still not legally recognized in many countries. However, same-sex couples still experience significant social marginalization and discrimination that force them to hide public manifestations of love and affection. The widespread opposition to homosexuality following the devastating spread of HIV, which was initially thought to be a consequence of deviant sexual behaviour, is just one of the many examples of rigidity in a social system that still discriminates against homosexual behaviour within friendships, school systems and in the work place and, not least, within the family itself. Their family of origin has also been a victim of discrimination, in part due to a pathological view of homosexuality that produced an attitude of blame and judgement towards the mother and father, the former being regarded as too symbiotic, the latter as too distant. Dysfunctional family relationships were identified as the cause of the "homosexual sickness" (La Sala, 1999). The American Psychological Association only removed homosexuality as a condition from the *Diagnostic and Statistical Manual of Mental Disorders* (DSM) in 1974.

The relationship between the heterosexual couple and the family of origin as a source of support and positive influence has been well researched by psychologists and family therapists. However, the literature dealing with homosexual men and women and their relationships with their own family of origin has been scarce and inadequate until recent years. Inadequate recognition and social prejudice contribute to the consolidation of negative convictions in many parents, reinforcing views that their children are wrong, or sick. However, today, the common consensus is that it is very beneficial and liberating for homosexuals and their families to reveal their sexual orientation and to live it openly. Despite this, many parents still tend to react with strong emotions, shame and disillusionment either when they discover that their son or daughter is homosexual, or when their children reveal it. This *coming out* often provokes a painful family crisis that can lead to a distancing between family members (La Sala, 2000). For homosexuals, the confession to the parents is described as the most difficult experience of their life. A son or daughter who declares his or her homosexuality may violently upset the family system at both an individual and interpersonal level. Mothers and fathers bring up their children taking their heterosexuality for granted. With a homosexual child, their dreams and plans about their children's marriage and the continuity of generations through the arrival of grandchildren are threatened. In spite of the very serious risk of disapproval, a high percentage of gays and lesbians make the decision to declare themselves to their parents, because they hope to increase the intimacy and honesty of their relationship with them. Coming out is a way of demonstrating to their partner and to themselves the commitment and desire to preserve their union.

Many homosexual couples have created stable unions that have lasted many years, debunking the stereotypical myth of the promiscuous homosexual, especially in reference to men who are always in search of new adventures. La Sala (2010) studied the influence of inter-generational disapproval on the homosexual couple's relationship, noting how the effort of revealing one's homosexuality seems to correlate with the process of differentiation of self, a fundamental step for establishing mature and emotionally significant relationships. As with heterosexual couples, sudden cut-off of one of the partners from their family of origin can have negative repercussions on the couple relationship, just as hiding or failing to reveal one's homosexuality does not allow for real autonomy, and can be considered instead an expression of a developmental impasse in the process of separation-individuation.

Finally, a current theme that cannot be ignored pertains to the issue of paternity and maternity of the same-sex couple. In the United States, about one-third of lesbians are mothers. But, there are many gay men who live with their children from previous relationships, or who are actively involved with the children they have fathered as donors to lesbian couples. Parenthood is an aspect of identity that homosexuals regard as important and demand to experience as a basic human right. The debate on this theme is rather heated and there are a multitude of opinions and studies around these issues (Patterson & D'Augelli, 2012; Golombok, 2015). Currently, many countries do not allow homosexual couples to marry or adopt children. More and more frequently, these couples go abroad to marry and to obtain reproductive assistance. Many studies have demonstrated that children's wellbeing is much more influenced by their relationships with their parents, their parents' sense of competence and security and the presence of social and economic support for the family than by the gender or the sexual orientation of their parents (Siegel & Perrin, 2013). Crouch, with his team at the University of Melbourne, surveyed 315 same-sex couples with a total of 500 children across Australia, and they pointed out that the main problem facing same-sex families was stigma (Crouch, Walters, McNair, Power and Davis, 2014). According to their studies, about two-thirds of children with same-sex parents experienced some form of stigma because of their parents' sexual orientation. Despite these kids receiving higher marks in physical health and social wellbeing, the stigma associated with their family structure ranged from subtle issues such as sending letters home from school addressed to "Mr" or "Mrs", to more harmful problems such as bullying at school. The greater the stigma a same-sex family faces, the greater the impact on a child's social and emotional wellbeing. Similar findings were highlighted in Golombok's (2015) recent studies and research, conducted for 35 years into "modern families" from around the world, stating that children are more likely to flourish in families that provide love, security and support, whatever their family structure.

To conclude, the ability to choose a partner because of love, in order to develop an intimate relationship based on affection, future planning, mutual trust and understanding, nowadays is considered a fundamental freedom of the individual, the basis for an open couple relationship that goes beyond sexual orientation, religion, skin colour, ethnicity or national origin.

References

Ahrons, C. A. (2007). Family Ties after Divorce. Long Term Implication for Children. *Family Process, 46*, 53–65.

Amato, P. R. (2000). The Consequence of Divorce for Adults and Children. *Journal of Marriage and Family, 62*, 1269–1287.

Andolfi, M. & Mascellani, A. (2013) *Teen Voices – Tales from Family Therapy*. San Diego: Wisdom Moon Publisher.

Andolfi, M., Mascellani A. & Santona, A. (Eds.) (2011). *Il Ciclo Vitale della Coppia Mista*. Milan: Franco Angeli.

Aquilino, W. S. (2006). The Noncustodial Father–Child Relationship from Adolescence into Young Adulthood. *Journal of Marriage and Family, 68*, 929–946.

Blau, M. (1993). *Families Apart: Ten Keys to Successful Co-parenting*. New York: Putman & Sons.

Bonvicini, M. L. (1992). *Immigrer au Féminin*. Paris : Ed. Ouvrières.

Boss, P. (2006). *Loss, Trauma and Resilience: Therapeutic Work with Ambiguous Loss*. New York: Norton.

Bray, J. H. & Kelly, J. (1998). *Stepfamilies: Love, Marriage and Parenting in the First Decade*. New York: Random House.

Brodzinsky, D. M. & Palacios, J. (Eds.) (2005). *Psychological Issues in Adoption, Research and Practice*. Santa Barbara, CA: Praeger Publisher.

Brodzinsky, D. M. & Schechter, D. (Eds.) (1993). *The Psychology of Adoption*. New York: Oxford University Press.

Carter, B. & McGoldrick, M. (Eds.) (2005). *The Expanded Family Life Cycle: Individual, Family and Social Perspective* (3rd ed.). New York: Pearson.

Chistolini, M. (2010). *La Famiglia Adottiva*. Milan: Franco Angeli.

Ciola, A. (1997). Stare Qui Stando Là (star Seduto fra due Sedie o la Condizione del Migrante). *Terapia Familiare*, 5, 21–28.

Crouch, S., Walters, E., McNair, R., Power, N. & Davis, N. (2014). Parent-Reported Measures of Child Health and Well-being in Same Sex Parent Families: a Cross Sectional Survey. *BMC Public Health*, 14, 1–12.

D'Andrea, A. (2001). *I Tempi dell'Attesa*. Milan: Franco Angeli.

Di Nicola, V. F. (1997). *A Stranger in the Family: Culture, Families, Therapy*. New York: Norton.

Goldscheider, F. & Sassler, S. (2006). Creating Stepfamilies: Integrating Children in the Study of Union Formation. *Journal of Marriage and Family*, 68, 275–291.

Golombok, S. (2015). *Modern Families. Parents and Children in New Family Forms*. Cambridge, MA: Cambridge University Press.

Greef, A. P. & Toit, C. D. (2009). Resilience in Remarried Families. *American Journal of Family Therapy*, 37, 114–126.

Hotvedt, M. (1997). Il Matrimonio Interculturale: l'Incontro Terapeutico. *Terapia Familiare*, 54, 55–66.

Jewett, C. L. (1978). *Adopting the Older Child*. Harvard, MA: Harvard Common Press.

King, V. (2009). The Family Formation: Implications for Adolescent Ties to Mothers, Nonresident Fathers and Stepfathers. *Journal of Divorce and Remarriage*, 71, 954–968.

Lambert, A. (2010). Stepparent Family Membership Status. *Journal of Divorce and Remarriage*, 51, 428–440.

La Sala, M. (1999). Coppie Omosessuali Maschili e Disapprovazione Intergenerazionale. In M. Andolfi (Ed.), *La Crisi della Coppia*. Milan: Raffaello Cortina, pp. 487–508.

La Sala, M. (2000). Lesbians, Gay Men and their Parents: Family Therapy for the Coming-out Crisis. *Family Process*, 39(1), 67–81.

La Sala, M. (2010). *Coming Out, Coming Home*. New York: Columbia University Press.

McGoldrick, M. & Hardy, K. V. (2008). *Re-Visioning Family Therapy: Race, Culture and Gender in Clinical Practice* (2nd ed.). New York: Guilford Press.

Mc Lanahan, S. & Carlson, M. S. (2004). Fathers in Fragile Families. In M. E. Lamb (Ed.), *The Role of the Fathers in Child Development*. Hoboken, NJ: Wiley, pp. 368–396.

Michaels, M. L. (2006). Factors that Contribute to Step Family Success: A Qualitative Analysis. *Journal of Divorce and Remarriage*, 44, 53–66.

Nelsen, J., Erwin, C. & Glenn, H. S. (1997). *Positive Discipline for Blended Families*. Rocklin, CA: Prima Publisher.

Papernow, P. L. (2009). *Becoming a Stepfamily*. New York: Routledge.

Patterson, C. J. & D'Augelli, A. R. (Eds.) (2012). *Handbook of Psychology and Sexual Orientation*. New York: Oxford University Press.

Roussel, L. (1989). *La Famille Incertaine*. Paris: Odile Jacob.

Scabini, E. & Regalia, C. (1993). La Famiglia in Emigrazione. Continuità e Fratture nelle Relazioni Intergenerazionali. *Terapia Familiare*, 43, 5–11.

Sewell, T. (1996). *Migrations and Cultures: A World View*. New York: Basic Books.

Siegel, B. & Perrin, E. (2013). Promoting the Well-being of Children whose Parents are Gay or Lesbian. *Pediatrics*, 4, 703–711.

Simon, R. J. & Altstein, H. (2002). *Adoption, Race and Identity*. New Brunswick, NJ: Transaction Publishing,

Steward, S. D. (2005). Boundary Ambiguity in Stepfamilies. *Journal of Family Issues*, 26, 1002–1029.

Sykes, M. R. (2001) Adopting with Contact: A Study of Adoptive Parents and the Impact of Continuing Contact with Families of Origin. *Journal of Family Therapy*, 23, 296–316.

Van Guiden, H. & Bartels-Rabb, L. M. (1993). *Real Parents, Real Children: Parenting the Adopted Child*. New York: Herder & Herder.

Visher, E. B. & Visher, J. S. (1991). *How to Win as a Stepfamily*. New York: Brunner-Mazel.

Volker, T., Terri, A. K. & Wetchler J. (Eds.) (2003). *Clinical Issues with Interracial Couples: Theories and Research*. Binghamton, NY: The Haworth Press.

Whiteman, T. (1993). *The Fresh Start Single Parenting Workbook*. Nashville, TN: Thomas Nelson.

4

FAMILY OBSERVATION METHODS

The study of family development represents a working model that has allowed us to embark on a journey beyond the individual. The inter-personal dimension, and the context within which relationships are formed, constitutes our main observation point. In order to know the individual better we need to understand his family history and frame personal problems within the parameters of his affective and relational world. In fact, these familial and social components have long been underestimated, both theoretically as well as in clinical practice, in favour of an observational model that exclusively focused on the inner self and the individual manifestations of psychopathology. Both the psychoanalytic tradition and the medical/psychiatric model have described and evaluated the client mostly as a monad, isolated from his relational components, thus running the risk of splitting the family unit into small segments.

The triad as a basic unit of observation

At the beginning of the 1960s, Bowen was the first to introduce the theoretical concept of triangles, regarding them as the basic structures of all relationships, including those that apparently involve only two people. The triangle is the way in which the emotional forces of every relational system are naturally organized and the dual relationship is a more restricted view of a wider relational system. The triad, as a basic unit of observation and understanding, is therefore considered as the place where the emotional and relational elements of the family system are played out. Many authors within the field of systemic theories have proposed the triangle as the unit of measurement of evolving family relationships (Minuchin, 1974; Haley, 1976; Bowen, 1978; Hoffman, 1981; Walsh, 1982; Andolfi, Angelo & De Nichilo,1989; Whitaker, 1989; Framo, 1992; Andolfi & Mascellani, 2013). By adopting the triad as the method of study of human relations, the observations about reality and psychopathology deeply differ from those made using the dyad as a lens. Consequently, the questions we ask family members during a therapeutic session will be triadic too, as will be described in a following chapter.

Triangulation as a relational modality

Closely related to the concept of triads is the notion of triangulation, which refers to the relational dynamics within emotional triads. The concept of triangulation differs greatly from the psychodynamic perspective to the systemic approach. In the psychodynamic model, the term refers to the experience of the oedipal child's exclusion from the parents' relationship, while in the systemic model it refers to the dysfunctional process where the child is caught in the parents' conflictual relationship in order to divert the tension between them. Various triadic hypotheses of relationships have been formulated over time by many authors who have studied pathological triangulation in families. In his article, "Toward a Theory of Pathological Systems", Haley (1977) proposed characteristics that need to be present to form a pathological triangulation called *perverse triad*. In this, a child is brought into a coalition with one parent against the other, who is disqualified in his/her role of parent, and this coalition might remain latent and denied at the explicit level. Incidentally, the main elements of Haley's perverse triad can be found in cases of *parental alienation syndrome,* where the alienating parent deprives the child of the nurturing of the vilified parent, especially in situations of very hostile marital separation, or when the vilified parent comes from another country and culture. Another dimension of triangulation is described as *favouritism,* when one parent favours one child at the expense of the other children. In this process, the other parent is cut off, indirectly alienated from the healthy and necessary evenhanded nurturing of all the children.

The study of triadic family structures was advanced by Minuchin, who was interested in triangulation, especially in relation to the detouring of marital conflict. Minuchin (1974) started from the hypothesis that children could be used to hide or detour conflict between the parents and from this premise he described four rigid configurations: triangulation, parent–child coalition, detouring–attack, detouring–support. Two parents, in open or covert conflict, who respectively try to attract the child's attention and support against the other, characterize *triangulation*. The situation places the child in a conflict of loyalty. In the *parent–child coalition*, there is a stable alliance of one parent with the child against the other parent. In the *detouring–attack* configuration, the parents join forces to control the destructive behaviour of the child, who becomes the scapegoat, even though they cannot agree on how to manage the child and behave in a disjointed manner. In the *detouring–support* configuration, the parents disguise their tensions by concentrating in a hyper-protective manner on a child who is identified as ill.

Selvini-Palazzoli, Cirillo, Selvini and Sorrentino (1989), in their book *Family Games,* later proposed two further dysfunctional triadic dynamics connected to the onset of serious psychotic symptomatology in the child, which they described as *instigation* and *relational deceit*. In the instigation scenario, a member of the triad is covertly forced into becoming the "strong arm" for another, only to find that the alliance is denied when the game is uncovered. In the relational deceit situation, a member of the triad is under the illusion of being part of a complicit relationship that is, in fact, revealed as only a strategic manoeuvre used to send messages to a third party.

Parentification has been well described by Minuchin (1974), Selvini Palazzoli, Boscolo, Cecchin and Prata (1978) and Andolfi et al. (1989) as a triadic dysfunctional structure, where a child assumes the role of caretaker over one or both parents who are unable to perform the expected nurturing roles and to carry out adult responsibilities. The parental child configuration is always the result of emotional abuse and, if persistent over time, can cause severe psychosomatic and relational problems in a child or adolescent. On the other hand, many parentified children might develop a great deal of resilience and in adulthood can become very competent and sensitive psychotherapists. As stated in previous publications (Andolfi et al., 1989; Andolfi & Mascellani 2013), the process of triangulation can also have a positive connotation when a third person can be the stimulus for discovering hidden personal or relational resources or for the evolution of the entire system. In triadic interactions, in fact, each of the participants can observe what happens between the other two, or can mediate or inform the others. For example, father and mother may argue because they have different opinions on a particular matter; the child can intervene in the discussion by adopting a less controversial attitude, thereby defusing the tension when the interaction becomes too intense. A parent can do the same thing when the other spouse argues with their child, making situations tolerable and productive. From this perspective, the presence of a third party becomes important to increase knowledge and facilitate intimacy, providing emotional support, especially during family transitions like the one brought about by the birth of a child, or after marital separation, a sudden loss or when children leave home. Relational triangles are thus understood as the elementary structure of all relationships, including those in which, on the surface, only two people are involved.

Tri-generational triangles

Tri-generational triangles are those relational triangles made up by members from three different generations. If a third dimension is added to the observation of family functioning, more complex aspects of current relationships and individual presenting problems are highlighted. For example, if a wife has a difficult relationship with her own mother or her husband, who fail to meet her emotional demands, these demands will probably be redirected towards the daughter. The daughter's relationship with the mother is therefore complicated by the presence of two super-imposed components: one that involves her directly and another in which she becomes the mediator of a demand initially directed to someone else (her maternal grandmother or her father).

Many inter-generational master family therapists have studied the family as an emotional system characterized by forces that lead to differentiation, and forces that tend to maintain a state of cohesion. It is within this model that family history, relationships with significant figures from the past and families of origin assume a central role. The framing of the family within an evolutionary and historical context has allowed us to place triadic relationships on a tri-generational level that encourages a more complex reinterpretation of the individual and her current relationships. The consideration of temporal and historic dimensions allows us to jump between the past, the present and the future, and to move between the grandparents, to the couple relationship and to that of the children. On the vertical axis are found attitudes, expectations, myths and fears that people grow up with and that are transmitted from one generation to the next following triadic paths. For example, in the male line of descent of grandfather–son–grandchild, professional achievements and success might be a value transmitted through generations. In the female line of descent, sacrificing for children might be an injunction that needs to be fulfilled in order to maintain loyalty to the female role. It could be said that these aspects of our life are like the deck of cards that were handed to us. The problem is what to do with them.

The introduction of the older generation in observing the parent–child relationship has therefore allowed us to observe the actual interactions among several people and gain a better understanding of the individual by using the resources that emerge once we move in and out of the present issues. To understand the individual fully, it is important to include the context in which she lives. The unit of observation cannot be the single individual, but must include the significant triadic relationships involving that person. Relational Psychology is based on the understanding of the family as an emotional system, where values, myths, loyalties and models of behaviour are transmitted and altered through generations.

The genogram: a graphic representation of family development

The genogram is a tool that maps the continuity of family generations and descendants through time. The connection with ancestors and lineage finds a representation in the image of a family tree, which symbolizes its ties with past, present and future generations (Andolfi, 1979; McGoldrick & Gerson, 1985; Montagano & Pazzagli, 1989). The search for family origins dates as far back as antiquity: the biblical world, characterized by detailed histories of lineages between races, is one example. The importance attributed to genealogy throughout history is based on the concept of belonging, especially in the inheritance of the land through centuries. The relevance of family ties is also clear in the literary world as, for example, in the most famous of Shakespearian tragedies, *Romeo and Juliet*, that tells the story of two unhappy lovers and the rivalry between two noble families from Verona during the early Middle Ages, the Montagues and the Capulets. In summary, the genogram is the graphic representation of the genealogical tree and a way for an individual to describe the historical development of his/her own family that includes at least the last three generations.

The relational therapist can utilize the genogram as a tool to gather information and enrich the client's verbal description through a graphic and visual representation of the family's emotional system. In the systemic-relational field, Bowen was a pioneer in the use of the genogram. Through the study of various families' genealogical trees going back from 100 to 300 years, he identified a transmission of family characteristics between one generation and the next, and he proved how it is possible to highlight different views of human phenomena by looking at family development in this way. In his famous paper entitled, "The Anonymous", described in his classic book *Family Therapy in Clinical Practice*, Bowen (1978) presented in great detail his own family genogram. He stressed the importance for therapists to work on their own family development as a way of learning how to engage better with families in therapy, and to avoid the risk of projecting on to clients their own family issues.

The genogram and its therapeutic function have been discussed by many authors, such as Guerin and Pendagast (1976), Andolfi (1979), Byng-Hall (1979), McGoldrick and Gerson (1985), Montagano and Pazzagli (1989) and Hellinger (2012), and became a standard and common instrument used by family therapists and counsellors for family assessment all over the world, in private practice as well as in institutional settings. The genogram includes names, symbols (square for male, circle for female), ages of all the family members, specific signs to indicate connections in each subsystem and between generations, dates and symbols for significant events (births, deaths, weddings, separations, abortion, etc.), information on occupation, education, cultural background, process of migration and cut-offs, and other relevant particulars.

It is important to note that, besides informing us on much family data, the drafting of the genogram permits the activation of emotions and intense memories in the presenter (whether we refer to a family member or to a supervisee), as well as deep reflections on important events and on their impact on the family emotional system. One very important aspect of this instrument is certainly that of allowing the observer to order data in a synthetic, clear and complete manner. Without this tool, it would be difficult to keep in mind the wide range of information relating to the family structure. However, what is certainly more important is the fact that the genogram allows us to see each person in the broader context of his/her family development. The genogram is useful in revealing missing information or data that is obscure. It helps to relive past experiences and brings back a series of memories, such as grief for important losses, different types of conflict and resentment in the context of the family of origin, in relationship to siblings, partners or ex-partners, allowing the discovery and redefinition of significant events and of the links that connect them. It is, in fact, through a triadic observation that each family member can be seen as an active participant in various triads. By outlining the configuration of the tri-generational network and identifying triangles, which have been emotionally overloaded, it becomes possible to understand the most complex aspects of current relationships.

How to use the genogram in therapy and consultation

The family genogram is a highly useful assessment tool as well as therapeutic device. Often, professionals in institutional settings discuss and make hypotheses about family functioning and individual psychopathology using the family genogram. Genograms produce the most fruit when a therapeutic relationship with the family has been formed. When family members start to trust the therapist and an alliance is established, the information they release becomes much more relevant and goes to the core of family problems.

The depression of Monica

The following example highlights the usefulness of genograms in therapy, in terms of producing relevant information. Monica, a woman in her 50s, came for therapy to treat her issue with long-term depression. The drawing of her family genogram was instrumental in highlighting the way in which the hostile separation of her parents had significant reverberations in the dynamics of the family. Her parents separated just one year after her marriage to Vinni, and the birth of their first child, Eleonora. The separation of her parents came at a crucial point in Monica's life and was a very painful experience for both her and her sister, Fabiola. Instead of creating a better connection between the sisters, the parents' separation increased their emotional distance and rivalry. Both sisters had competed for their mother's affection and care since their childhood and this continued into their adulthood. Monica tried to involve her mother in her negative moods, and the triad made up of the mother and two daughters was full of tension and past resentments, with the total exclusion of the father Giuseppe, who was accused of being responsible for the marital separation because of his macho attitude towards women. The two sisters were so busy getting their mother's attention that they did not protect their marriages. So, one after the other, the marriages ended badly, leaving them as single parents with a lot of difficulties and conflicts in raising their own children. The genogram provided a quick and easy access to many profound family events and conflictual relationships, spanning over three generations.

In the last 20 years, I have changed my way of using the genogram in therapy. In my own work, I prefer to ask the family to draw the genogram early in therapy, even in the first session. This becomes a creative way to do an assessment, but is also a powerful tool to establish a therapeutic bond. In my child–centred approach, I empower the problematic child or adolescent by involving her as a natural co-therapist, asking her to draw the family genogram with the help of the other family members (Andolfi, 1994). This transforms the identified client into a competent person who can draw and describe family events. Parents are usually very pleased to see this competence and are happy to collaborate by providing important data.

It does not matter if the child does not follow the graphic rules in building the genogram. The result is a very creative and special drawing, and the therapist plays the role of an explorer, curious to know more about family members and events. It is amazing to see how children and adolescents become family historians, asking their parents several questions about their own childhood, the way in which grandparents educated and cared for and disciplined them, on important events like losses, cut-offs in the family and so on.

The yellow symbol of Fatma

Before a live family consultation, the therapist who works with the family usually presents and discusses the family genogram with his own colleagues and me. It is my customary practice to work with the family using this genogram, engaging children and adults by asking them to explain different aspects of it and completing it if there is missing or wrong information. I often say, "This is a graphic representation of your family: who better than you to accompany me through your family's life history?" In one consultation, a therapist prepared a very detailed genogram. Fatma, a young Tunisian girl with a severe phobia, was represented by a circle coloured in solid yellow to highlight that she was the identified client in the family. White signs symbolized the other family members – white squares for men and white circles for women. In order to highlight the problematic position she held in her family, I started the session by playing symbolically with this yellow label, saying to the girl: "This is your label; you are all yellow because you are different from everybody else." I then encouraged her to take me inside her family story in order to find, together, other "yellow signs", to symbolize other problems in the family. In the space of an hour, we discovered so many other problems and dramas in previous generations that I was able to say to her: "Your yellow circle looks so small at the end of the session while at the beginning it seemed like the big problem of the family". She looked at me feeling very reassured and supported, and said: "You are right!" The therapist and the other family members were able to gain fresh understanding and insight into the family history and dynamics, and the way in which Fatma had been scapegoated as the problem in the family.

John, Liz and the photographic genogram

The use of family photos is also a powerful tool in therapy. I would like to illustrate the use of family photos in therapy by recounting a session with a family I consulted with a few years ago in Denmark. John and Liz, a middle-aged couple, Liz's parents and John's mother, as well as their therapist and myself attended the session. Liz had been depressed for a number of years. John was a very busy and sporty man who tried to avoid conflict as much as possible. They had three kids and the marriage was in deep crisis, apparently because of her depression. At the start of the session, I asked Liz if their children knew about this meeting and then I invited her to show me the pictures of her children. Very proudly, she opened her wallet and showed me four photos, one next to the other, of her husband and the three kids individually. During the session, it emerged that she had always taken care of John like a supportive and protective mother, until more recent years when she became fed up with this role. From the role of a caring mother, she moved to the position of a lonely wife, with no emotional support from her husband, and the depression served to mask the lack of intimacy in the couple. Using the photos as a metaphor for change, I suggested that Liz find another position for John's photo in her wallet, distant from the children so that he would no longer look like the fourth child in the row! Even more interesting was to discover that John had only one picture in his wallet, which he showed me with great pleasure: a photo of Liz when they first met, a very attractive young woman at 19 years of age! It was easy to remark that he wanted to remember that Liz he had fallen in love with, rather than to appreciate the mature wife of today. Playing with the photos of the couple generated high levels of engagement and encouraged everybody to move closer to the table in the middle of the room and to show their own photos. Liz's parents proudly showed a photo of their 40th wedding anniversary and of their grand-children, while John's mother, very moved, showed us the picture of the beloved husband she had lost a few years earlier. Family relationships and main events were all present on the table, vividly and clearly, through this spontaneous photographic genogram, which proved to be much more valuable therapeutically than extensive verbal explanations.

How to use the genogram in training therapists

For many years at the University of Rome, I have been teaching Family Clinical Psychology to graduate students. I encouraged them to learn about family systems, not only through theoretical lectures, but also through the presentation of their own family genograms in class. I asked them to describe one or two relevant family events, and to identify triadic emotional connections in their family of origin. It was amazing to see how much more they were learning about family development by using their own personal experiences. The same teaching principle has been applied in the post-graduate training of family therapists in the Accademia di Psicoterapia della Famiglia in Rome, by directing trainees to learn how to work with families by presenting their own family genograms. This very moving and sometimes pain-ful experience can produce cognitive and emotional shifts in awareness. Presenting one's own family is not just a descriptive matter; rather, it recreates a symbolic trip back into experiences or into areas of family secrets, obscure events or unfinished business, which have been transmitted through stories and anecdotes from one gen-eration to another. Often there is one side of the genogram described as full of life, caring and with relational resources while the other side is silent, or less known, or perceived as negative. The function of the teacher, together with the training group, is to challenge, through the use of relational questioning, some areas of rigid-ity or prejudice deeply rooted in the presenter's mind in order to offer some new opening and reframing of family events and relational patterns. This experience not only increases the level of self-awareness of the presenter, but it also represents a model of exploration that he/she can use in working with families in therapy.

The photographic genogram is a very good application of this too. Trainees are asked to select and bring to the meeting some of the most relevant photos of their family, including photographs of grandparents and siblings, and especially pictures of the past when they were small children. Photographs have such an evocative quality, able to activate special moods and memories, which will increase the understanding of family development through time. Another useful application of this tool is for therapists to assess where they have, consciously or unconsciously, positioned themselves in their depiction of the genogram of the family in treatment. Many therapists use the genogram to focus on family issues, but often forget to consider where they are positioned with relation to the family in treatment. A very relevant question to address to a therapist in supervision is, "Where are you in this genogram?" By identifying themselves with the letter T in the genogram, therapists can indicate where they feel they are positioned, and by doing so highlight their position in the therapeutic process. Therapists might be very close to the identified client or to the controlling mother or, on the contrary, might have a sense of balanced distance from each member of the family. The standpoint of the therapist highlights both the quality of the therapeutic process and the inter-subjective nature of family exploration.

Family sculpture: a powerful tool for systemic therapists

Family sculpture was introduced into family and couple therapy by Virginia Satir in the late 1960s, and consists of a non-verbal, visual and spatial representation of family/marital relationships. The sculptor (a family member or a therapist) is asked to create a sculpture by placing each person in the room according to a chosen degree of closeness and distance from the other family members. Each person is given specific bodily positions, gestures and movements, in order to represent different moods (happiness, sadness, withdrawal isolation), and emotional connections/disconnections. Important absent or dead family members can also be included in this symbolic portrayal, which has a very intense, evocative power. Once people have been positioned in the sculpture, they are requested to hold their positions and remain silent for a few seconds. After this non-verbal representation, each person, including the sculptor, is asked to provide feedback on the emotions experienced in their specific role. This second part is very important because it allows for a very intense and authentic sharing of deep personal and relational feelings.

This powerful non-verbal tool has been described by various authors, in different settings, with different meanings and variations (Satir, 1967; Duhl, Kantor & Duhl, 1973; Papp, Silverstein & Carter, 1973; Constantine, 1978; Banmen, 2002; Haber, 2002; Hellinger, 2012). In Europe, I introduced family sculpting, after personal experience in learning this technique from Peggy Papp and Kitty Laperriere, at the Ackerman Family Therapy Institute, New York, in the early 1970s. I described family sculpting in my first book, *Family Therapy: An Interactional*

Approach (Andolfi, 1979), and different forms of sculpting were further elaborated by Caillé (1990) and Onnis et al. (1994).

In summary, family sculpture is considered a form of art therapy, where family relationships are represented in a very dramatic fashion without the use of words. While the genogram is based on a verbal description of family histories, the family sculpture privileges the analogic model of communication and, through body language, the more implicit and deeper emotions are explored, thereby side-stepping the defensive barrier of verbal expressions. The intensity of the experience elicited by family sculpture enables each person to see different connections, to feel new emotions, to listen and to be heard. It increases self-esteem and generates more authenticity in looking at relational problems, that goes beyond the defensive verbal barrier and the frequent mechanism of "double thinking" before answering questions. Sculpting therefore is both a powerful assessment device as well as a special tool to engage couples and families in the therapeutic process. However, in order to use it properly, it is necessary to have established a solid alliance with family members. Limiting therapy to merely talking as a modality to learn about the family results in a much less personal and relational exposure.

Family sculpture in therapy

I have been using family sculpture in therapy for more than 40 years with families, couples and individual clients. I experimented with an incredible number of variations of this non-verbal representation of family relationships, moving across different stages of family life cycle. I have also used sculptures in training groups, especially when working with "professional handicaps" (Haber, 1990), as I will describe later in this chapter.

Going back to the past

Sculpting allows for the re-enacting of memories and images that remain very vivid in the family narrative over a three-generational dimension. For example, in the presence of the family of origin at the session, the therapist can ask a father, who is worried for his own children, to sculpt family relationships at a particular moment, when he was a young child. He will go back, through the act of remembering, to when he was eight years old, at a very dramatic moment in family life, sculpting himself in the action of protecting his mother from her violent husband. He might sculpt the triad made up of himself, standing in the middle with both hands open, representing his intention to protect his mother, who is looking down and scared, and his father, in a very aggressive stance and facial expression. The purpose of this dramatization is to recreate, in a safe context, a replica of past tensions and deep family pain in order to unload the emotional weight carried by the child many years earlier, which is still present in the "family script". This may allow for the transformation of family patterns and paves the way for inter-generational reconciliation. For his children, this might help them to understand more clearly the pain and difficulties experienced by their father at their age, and to gain a more complete picture of him.

In the present moment

In another therapeutic situation, a middle-aged woman who felt totally unsafe and neglected in her family during her entire childhood was finally able to cry and release her long-term pain by sculpting an ideal image of a mother–child relationship in the presence of her mother. In her sculpture, she sat on her mother's knees, like a two-year-old, and directed her mother to hold her and gently caress her hair. The mother's hug and care in the present moment had a very healing effect on their intimate relationship and had the power of repairing an old wound. Sculpting often allows for a very positive experience of regression and, as is possible, through temporal jumps, symbolically to go back and imagine a different childhood.

In couple therapy

Sculpting can be used in couple therapy as an assessment tool as each partner could be asked to represent how s/he perceives the relationship. It is amazing to see how surprised each of them may be by the image chosen by the other partner to describe their relationship, as they generally find it difficult to put themselves in the other person's shoes.

The dance of the exclusion

In one session, a wife made a very simple and powerful sculpture by asking the husband to stand next to the door, looking out, and putting herself seated in the centre of the room, looking down with a feeling of total loneliness. During the feedback session, he expressed a sense of deep anger towards the wife for placing him so far away, and making him feel totally disconnected! However, the wife said that she had chosen that position for him because he was always emotionally distant from her, and she felt much neglected, waiting for him to notice her. As a result, the sculpture opened up the issue of both clients feeling equally rejected, and the need to redefine their position, and discover their mutual desire to care for each other and to be taken care of. After several years of rigid complementarity, there is often a reciprocal dance of rejection in the relationship. Sculpting can be a very powerful tool to ignite fresh insight in therapy and can help to transform roles and discover healthier patterns of communication and understanding. Sculpting can also highlight negative dynamics in couple and family dynamics.

The marital tortures

In another case, a couple that had been experiencing entrenched and long-term conflict sculpted what they described as "marital tortures". The wife sculpted herself lying down, face up, protecting her body with an overturned chair placed on top of her, while the husband was pushing a pen, like a stick, in one of her ears. During therapy, she often referred to her husband torturing her by talking all the time and giving her little chance to reply. The husband, who always felt rejected by his wife, especially in their sex life, sculpted her standing in the middle of the room while he covered her from top to toe with toilet paper, like a mummy. Sculpting the most wounded aspects of a relationship is a powerful way to make visible the main issues in a relationship, in a very concrete way. It allows the therapist to enter into the marital drama, and hopefully help them to overcome it.

A sculpture of the future

As already, discussed, temporal jumps allow family members and couples to reconnect with experiences of the past and to understand its link to present issues and dynamics. It is equally useful to propose a sculpture of the future: that is, to imagine how relationships might be in the future, especially in relation to significant family events. It could be an image of the family facing the imminent death of a significant member, a beloved child leaving home, the process of migrating or changing jobs and so on. All kinds of fears, cut-offs and expectations for the future can be represented and elicit a number of insights and suggestions to families as well as to therapists.

Sculpting in individual therapy

Moving to non-verbal experiences is always useful because verbal channels of communication are often littered with reiteration of each person's problem storyline, which in turn increases people's defences. A person can talk about feeling the burden of a certain job or fearing the loss of a family member or the ending of a marriage, but it is very different when the therapist asks the client to show it, using her body to represent it by assuming certain gestures and positions or looking in a certain way. It is like creating a self-portrait, and condenses into an image a powerful set of emotions and deep-seated feelings. By doing this with the guidance and assistance of the therapist, the therapeutic alliance is deepened, because the experience is shared and the reverberations of its positive effects are often long-lasting.

Sculpting in supervision and in the personal training of the therapist

As already described, the genogram is often used as a way to present a clinical case in group supervision. While verbal information provided to describe individual symptoms and family development is essential and helpful, sculpting can illuminate a very different way of understanding the family and provide fresh insights into the case. Verbal information speaks from the level of our intellect, our head, while sculpting allows us to move from our head to our gut, our intuitive perceptions about the family. The verbal description might be very articulate, providing much data and details of family events, while sculpting family relationships is immediate and synthetic. It selects a chosen and defined area of observation. Probably the biggest difference regards the position of the therapist. The presentation of a family genogram can be done with very little or no personal involvement on the part of the therapist, whilst sculpting requires an active, creative engagement by the therapist. She has to choose what to represent, has to apportion family roles to colleagues (who will play father, mother, identified client, etc.), and put them in the sculpture according to her own perception of family relationships. At the end of the representation, the therapist will receive important feedback from each member of the group who took part in the sculpture. They will discuss their felt experience of their role in the sculpture. This exercise enlarges the therapist's vision of the dynamics in the family, helping to shift any rigid or negative opinions about family members. The therapist can also be asked by the supervisor to create a second sculpture, this time including herself as the therapist in relation to the family. This exercise illuminates her position in the therapeutic system. This exercise stimulates self-reflection on the inter-subjective nature of the therapeutic process. Sculpting herself in the family system is a very intense and powerful experience, which bypasses any professional defences, and helps the therapist to experience, from the inside and more directly, the family's relationships and individual problems and to feel closer to the family's pain and to their hopes.

Sculpting professional handicaps

For over 35 years, I have been organizing special intensive courses for international colleagues, focusing on the interplay between professional and personal issues that I refer to as "professional handicaps". Therapists often experience recurring themes that create a therapeutic impasse in their work. Common themes expressed by therapists include: "I don't know how to work with people who present with violent behavior"; "I tend to protect children from bad parents in the session"; "I'm very sensitive to mothers' depression"; "I don't know how to engage fathers in therapy if they are very uninvolved"; "I don't know how to feel empathy for a violent husband"; and "I don't know how to engage small children in therapy".

Once a therapist has identified issues where he experiences a blockage, I explore how this may be linked to unfinished business or active resonances in his own family. I invite the therapist to create a sculpture related to his own family development, using group members to play family roles, in order to represent blockages, cut-offs, painful separations, child neglect, sudden losses and so on. At the end of this experiential work, the parallel process between the personal and professional issues of the therapist often becomes clear and visible. The links between the difficulties experienced with families in therapy, the issues and the projections related to active personal family conflicts and unfinished business will be illuminated. Different sculptures have been created using this very special form of art therapy, sometimes even bizarre ones. For example, one therapist felt blocked in not knowing how to explore the client's cultural background. I asked him first to create a sculpture that captured his own experience of migration from one country to another and his contrasting cultural identities. The therapist can choose colleagues to sculpt with body postures the two different countries and show the emotional distance and disconnection between them. Learning about his own cultural ambivalence helped the therapist to move more easily through his client's cultural dilemmas.

In another situation, a therapist had difficulty integrating her ideas with her feelings and presented with psychosomatic responses in stressed situations. The therapist was asked to create a sculpture to show how her different organs and body parts were disconnected. The sculptor chose group members to play her head, heart, lungs and guts. She was directed to give action and movement to each organ, illustrating the lack of harmony, in the same way she might sculpt her clients' dysfunctional relationships.

The aim of all these dramatizations is to allow therapists to be more aware of their own personal emotional triggers and reactions in working with problematic families and to gain more self-confidence and insight in dealing with clients, as well as promoting personal growth. The training group is a great resource in sculpting, because it offers emotional containment and a safe place for personal exposures. It also fulfills a healing function, due to the colleagues' verbal and non-verbal reflections of the roles they played in the sculpture.

Role-playing in therapy and training

With its roots in Moreno's psychodrama, role-playing in family and couple therapy is an exceptional tool for families and clients struggling with a variety of issues. When given the chance to "act" in an unfamiliar role, whether as self or others, new ideas and feelings can be uncovered. Taking on a different persona, exploring unfamiliar motives and gestures, seeing different patterns of interactions among family members is fascinating. It is a great way to gain insight into oneself and others, becoming more sensitive to the viewpoints and needs of significant family members or one's own partner. In couple therapy it might be very useful to ask each partner to change chairs and roles and, for a short time, to play the part of the other one, either through words or body language. The therapist can join in and occasionally take the role of the identified patient or family member who is worried or suffering because of problems with the children. This simple and sometimes enjoyable technique can generate significant insights, and the therapist can learn how it feels to be "in other people's shoes". A role can be played with words and through actions and body postures.

Two very angry little children

On one occasion, the mother of two little Afro-American children brought them to therapy against their will because of their bad behaviour. They were dressed up in suits and ties, and looked very angry and mutinous. Instead of trying to engage them directly and run the risk of failing, I joined with them by mimicking their body expressions and their mood. I donned a tie and a jacket like them, sat next to them, looked directly ahead with an angry face in total silence. After a while, I said, "It is very tough to be forced to go to see somebody instead of playing with friends". At this, they both turned their heads toward me, curious and smiling, which then allowed me to say, "How can I help you today?" Joining in with the children in this manner allowed me to break through their anger and defences that could have blocked therapy.

A special consultation with two empty chairs

During my clinical experience, I have worked extensively with couples where partners were psychologists and psychiatrists, who came to therapy to deal with major conflicts, often paralysed by mutual anger and competition. I once saw two very competent marital therapists who were doing a very poor job with their own relationship. I suggested a special session in which I put in front of them two empty chairs which would represent each of them and their difficult relationship as a couple. Sitting in front of these chairs, the three of us, professionals, had to find a solution to help this couple in crisis. I played the role of the consultant and they were acting as two marital therapists. By splitting them into two teams, the "couple client" and the "couple of expert therapists", I allowed them to have a different perspective on their marital crisis by using their own professional expertise. It was like a session of direct supervision and the suggestions we gave the "clients" were very appropriate and accurate. We had a lot of fun creating a very paradoxical simulation and they were able to take all those insights home.

Role-playing family dynamics, generally described as a family simulation, has a very long tradition in the training of systemic family therapists (Donini et al., 1987). It has also been a fantastic tool to teach younger therapists how to work with families presenting a variety of personal and relational difficulties. Role-playing is a playful, representational technique that implies an element of fiction. It facilitates the dramatization, in words and actions, of desires, needs, fears and painful experiences in the family life cycle. It can be a way of highlighting how to work effectively with clients as well as a way of demonstrating the application of theory in action. The first simulated family was played in the late 1950s by Bateson, Jackson, Haley and Weakland at the Mental Research Institute in Palo Alto, California. They observed that impersonating the roles of the members of a family provokes a strong emotional involvement about the behaviour of the people represented by them. Satir noticed that people had enormous capacity to assume certain roles in a simulated family group and, in so doing, highlighted their capacity for change. As with sculpting, at the end of a simulated family session, it is very important to allow each "actor" to reflect and share with the group the range of deep emotions and thoughts experienced in the given role during role-playing (Satir, Banmen, Gerber & Gomori, 2006).

References

Andolfi, M. (1979). *Family Therapy: An Interactional Approach*. New York: Plenum Press.

Andolfi, M. (1994). The Child as Co-Therapist. In M. Andolfi & R. Haber (Eds.) *Please, Help Me With This Family*. New York: Brunner/Mazel, pp. 73–89.

Andolfi, M. & Mascellani, A. (2013). *Teen Voices. Tales of Family Therapy*. San Diego: Wisdom Moon Publishing.

Andolfi, M., Angelo, C. & De Nichilo, M. (1989). *The Myth of Atlas: Families and the Therapeutic Story*. New York: Brunner/Mazel.

Banmen, J. (2002). The Satir Model: Yesterday and Today. *Contemporary Family Therapy*, 24, 7–22.

Bowen, M. (1978). *Family Therapy in Clinical Practice*. New York: Jason Aronson.

Byng-Hall, J. (1979). Re-editing Family Mythology during Family Therapy. *Journal of Family Therapy*, 1(2), 103–116.

Caillé, P. (1990). *Il Rapporto Famiglia-Terapeuta. Lettura Sistemica di una Interazione*. Rome: NIS.

Constantine, L. (1978). Family Sculpture and Relationship Mapping Techniques. *Journal of Marriage and Family Counseling*, 4, 13–23.

Donini, G., De Santis, S., Galante, L. C., Michelis, P., Massimilla, M. & Mormile M. C. (1987). Il Role-Playing Tramite Sedute Familiari Simulate. *Terapia Familiare*, 25, 49–61

Duhl, F., Kantor, D. & Duhl, B. (1973). Learning, Space and Action in Family Therapy. In D. A. Bloch (Ed.), *Techniques of Family Psychotherapy*. New York: Grune and Stratton.

Framo, J. L. (1992). *Family of Origin. An Intergenerational Approach*. New York: Routledge.

Guerin, P. J. & Pendagast, E. G. (1976). Evaluation of Family System and Genogram. In P. J. Guerin (Ed.), *Family Therapy: Theory and Practice*. New York: Gardner Press.

Haber, R. (1990). From Handicap to Handi-caple. Training Systemic Therapists in use of Self. *Family Process*, 29, 375–384.

Haber, R. (2002). Virginia Satir; An Integrated Humanistic Approach. *Contemporary Family Therapy*, 24, 23–34.

Haley, J. (1976). *Problem-Solving Therapy*. San Francisco: Jossey-Bass.

Haley, J. (1977). Toward a Theory of Pathological Systems. In P. Watzlawick & J. H. Weakland (Eds.), *The Interactional View*. New York: Norton, pp. 31–49.

Hellinger, B. (2012). *Family Constellations Revealed*. Antwerp, Belgium: Indra Torsten Preiss.

Hoffman, L. (1981). *Foundations of Family Therapy: A Conceptual Framework for System Change*. New York: Basic Books.

McGoldrick, M. & Gerson, R. (1985). *Genograms in Family Assessment*. New York: Norton.

Minuchin, S. (1974). *Families and Family Therapy*, Cambridge, MA: Harvard University Press.

Montagano, S. & Pazzagli, A. (1989). *Il Genogramma. Teatro di Alchimie Familiari*. Milan: Franco Angeli.

Onnis, L., Di Gennaro, A., Cespa, G., Agostini, B., Chouhy, A., Dentale, R. C. & Quinzi P. (1994). Sculpting Present and Future: a Systemic Intervention Model Applied to Psychosomatic Families. *Family Process*, 33(3), 341–355.

Papp, P., Silverstein, O. & Carter, E. (1973). Family Sculpting in Preventive Work with Well Families. *Family Process,* 12(2), 197–212.

Satir, V. (1967). *Conjoint Family Therapy: A Guide to Theory and Technique*. Palo Alto, CA: Science and Behavior Books.

Satir, V., Banmen, J., Gerber, J. & Gomori, M. (2006). *The Satir Model: Family Therapy and Beyond*. Palo Alto, CA: Science and Behavior Books,

Selvini Palazzoli, M., Boscolo, L., Cecchin, G. & Prata, G. (1978). *Paradox and Counter-paradox: A New Model in the Therapy of the Family in Schizophrenic Transactions*. New York: Jason Aronson.

Selvini Palazzoli, M., Cirillo, S., Selvini, M. & Sorrentino, A. M. (1989). *Family Games: General Models of Psychotic Processes in the Family*. New York: Norton.

Walsh, F. (Ed.) (1982). *Normal Family Processes*. New York: Guilford Press.

Whitaker, C. A. (1989). *Midnight Musings of a Family Therapist*. New York: Norton.

5

TOWARD AN ASSESSMENT OF FAMILY FUNCTIONING

The three-storey house

A systemic-relational assessment attempts to observe individual behaviour and symptomatology within the complex dynamics underlying human relationships. Its purpose is to understand the processes that influence the development of individuals' identity and personality within the relational contexts they are a part of, starting with the family but extending the focus to include schools, friendships, work environments and, not least, the larger community. Relational observation therefore tries to connect presenting complaints and problems, especially the ones manifested by children and adolescents, to relevant family events by observing the link between past traumas, family cut-off, marital crises, sudden losses and the client's present actions. Therefore we pay attention to the complex family architecture that is a result as much of the past (ancestral generations), as of the present and future (expectations and plans).

A good starting point to reflect on family evolution is in the formation of a couple. Whitaker (1989) wrote that each marriage (the couple relationship) represents the effort of merging two cultures into one and is the result of an "implicit contract" between two families. Whether the families are explicitly and consciously involved in the formulation of this contract makes no difference. With the formation of the couple, both the two partners bring with them the cultural baggage from their family of origin, and from that moment, they begin a long and arduous attempt at integration and mediation of the *dowries* brought by the spouses. This family inheritance is not always appreciated and shared by one or the other partner. Nevertheless, it is almost inevitable that it will exercise a powerful influence in their lives. Couple formation, therefore, is not just the beginning of a new family. It is the continuation of two separate storylines that will intersect each other, giving birth to a new family narrative.

To formulate a relational assessment a multi-generational lens will be needed and the metaphor of a three-storey house will help to understand family dynamics. Let us imagine that the parental couple occupies the middle floor, the children inhabit the ground floor and the family of origin is on the top floor. The inhabitants of each of the floors are distinguishable by age, generational identities, distinct verbal and body language, different life experiences and responsibilities, different ways of dealing and remembering life events, ideas on planning the future and ways of living in the present. For the family members, moving from one floor to the next allows them to enter a different world from their own. The generational gap indicates the sense of integral inter-generational differences that operates at a personal, familial and social level through time. However, we also need to observe the horizontal axis of the couple and sibling relationships, and how they influence and are influenced by the vertical axis of grandparents and children. To formulate a relational assessment it becomes necessary for the therapist to widen the observational lens, shifting attention from one floor to the next, performing "temporal jumps" and carefully watching the quality of inter-generational boundaries and the strength of the "we-ness" of the couple, which is based on the quality of their attachment bonding (Johnson, 2004). Most psychopathology manifested in the younger generation is a direct consequence of the boundary invasion, confusion and inversion described by Minuchin (1972) in his outstanding *Structural Theory*.

Differences in couple's configurations

Exploring the couple dyad means entering the most vulnerable area of the entire family structure, which is often burdened by increasing responsibilities, inter-generational collusion and partial or incomplete separation from the respective families of origin. Different cultural and educational models and specific ways of planning and organizing life also challenge it. Each member of the couple are each other's partners but, at the same time, they are children in relation to their parents and, once they start their own family, become parents themselves. This network of functions and roles is structured along two axes, a vertical one with different hierarchical levels (grandparents, parents, children) and a horizontal one represented by relationships of equal hierarchical level –spouses, siblings, friends (Andolfi, 1999; Andolfi, Falcucci, Mascellani, Santona & Sciamplicotti, 2006; Andolfi & Mascellani, 2012). A relational therapist, therefore, cannot limit the observation to only one level, such as exploring the quality of the couple relationship or parent–child interactions. It is important to widen the horizon to observe how the family organization evolves over time and through generations. We have identified four main types of couple functioning according to how the formation and development of the couple have been influenced by the quality of inter-generational bonds, which also affect the way in which the couple can confront parenthood. Couple configurations differ according to the degree that the couple is balanced or unbalanced, in relation to the process of personal differentiation of each partner from parents and family of origin. These typologies are useful as a general schema, but obviously, they represent only the extremes of a continuum given by the increasing or decreasing level of autonomy and of emotional individuation that characterize the members of every single family. Couples can also be "sandwiched" between the older generation and that of the children.

The harmonious couple

Two partners, who are able to share and respect each other in a very intimate and reliable relationship, are depicted as the harmonious couple. Both partners have been able to individuate fully from their respective families of origin; what belongs to the past (expectations, myths, traditions, principles) does not invade the couple's space and territory, but represents a precious value that each partner brings to the relationship, as a kind of affective dowry. A harmonious couple has therefore achieved an adequate balance between belonging and separation. There is harmonious connection between each of the partners and their family of origin, without significant interference between past ties and the couple's present relationship. Both partners describe their developmental processes within their own family in a positive way, without undue pressure or interference from the previous generations. At the same time, they are able to see their family critically and to maintain their independence while respecting family connections. They have succeeded in completing the developmental stage of children and have assumed new roles and responsibilities (as spouse, parent), with recognition and legitimization from their own family of origin. They have healthy and positive relationships with their siblings because there were no negative triangulations when they were children.

The high-conflict couple

High-conflict couples are often encountered in therapy due to the toxic levels of tension and pain they experience in their daily life. This type of couple experiences entrenched and ongoing conflict on multiple levels. It is common for them to develop a parent–child relational modality and we frequently observe that the couple's connection is profoundly influenced by the unresolved problems in their respective families of origin. Typically, one partner has not really separated from his or her family of origin, but has experienced an early emotional cut-off in that s/he has run away from any kind of emotional and physical connection with the family of origin, although the person is still angry and hurt because of the unfinished business with parents and siblings. The other partner, in contrast, has failed to individuate from his or her own family, with whom s/he is greatly enmeshed. The result is often that the couple will be adopted by the family of the undifferentiated spouse, because neither one nor the other is able to nurture and protect their couple unit from intrusion by the family of origin; one is too involved and the other too distant. In fact, the partner who was emotionally deprived of early positive attachment figures might unconsciously enjoy the dependence on the other's family to compensate for the lack of care in his or her own family.

The unstable couple

Unstable couples are formed by two very insecure and lonely people, who experienced similar conditions of neglect or detachment from their own families, in which the attraction between the partners seems strongly centred on their mutual deprivation of care. In an attempt to satisfy each other's unmet needs from their family of origin in terms of attachment, affection and direction, they unconsciously need the other to become the parent they never had, thus creating considerable confusion about the expectations and requests within the couple. This dynamic does not generate real couple intimacy and complicity, but rather a continuous demand for presence and proximity that limits the freedom of both partners, because it is the result of their mutual inability to tolerate distance. Lack of security and instability are the main ingredients in this type of couple, where both partners act as if they are orphans even when their parents are still alive, but are not emotionally available to them. The condition we described as *psychosocial orphans* is very painful and, eventually, this unstable couple will search for reassurance. If it is not forthcoming from upstairs (the older generation), or worse still, from their couple relationship, they will try to get it from downstairs (their children). It is not difficult to understand that a child brought into the world to fill a void is deprived prematurely of the authentic care and nurture required to grow safely.

The "sandwiched" couple, caught between two generations

The social phenomenon of increasing longevity in the world today has given birth to new and unplanned relational modalities that significantly influence the couple's dynamics. The older generation is ever more often present at the development of the couple and in the grandchildren's upbringing. There are generally three categories of the elderly. In the first set, we have elderly people who are in good health, are able to appreciate the value of age and are free to enjoy this phase of life on both personal and social levels. In the second set, we have elderly people who function primarily as babysitters for their families. They find fulfilment in their role of grandparents, are engaged full-time in the emotional care and education of the grandchildren and are an invaluable resource for the parents. This is even more so in a situation of couple separation, where they can become an essential point of reference for family life. In the third set, we have the elderly who are sick or mentally unwell. Taking care of elderly parents when they become incapacitated is a very onerous undertaking, often over many years, both on the emotional and organizational fronts, for the couple. Care for this set of the elderly population can differ widely according to various cultural traditions. Western communities often rely on support structures such as nursing homes or the use of home care workers. Eastern communities, in contrast, tend to feel that they have to care for the elderly at home, requiring great sacrifices from the younger generations. In both cases, the pressure of caring for elderly family members can be great, either in terms of organizing the professional care or in being slaves in the fulfilment of this duty.

This pressure on the couple from the generation above is exacerbated when adult children delay moving out to live independent lives of their own. This increasingly more frequent phenomenon is especially experienced in those countries where there is an economic crisis and job shortages. In these cases, we are faced with a situation defined as the *crowded nest*, which is the opposite of the evolutionary experience of families in other socio-economic contexts, where the exit of young people from the family corresponds to the *empty-nest* phase. In the empty-nest phase, couples need to rediscover a new understanding and affective equilibrium after years of focusing predominantly on the care and upbringing of the children. Otherwise, they might run the risk, once the children have gone, of not finding any reason to stay together. For many contemporary couples, however, even at the age of 50 or 60, it can become increasingly difficult to maintain a lively and vital intimate space because they are caught between two forces that compress them: the older generation from above and the children from below. This phenomenon is known as the sandwiched couple (Andolfi & Mascellani, 2013).

Social assessment of couple functioning

It might be useful to focus attention on the couple's social development too, that is to say, the extra-familial dimension of their relationship. The first parameter to take into consideration is the couple's system of friendships. In harmonious couples, the two partners happily share friends. Those friendships that are more personal to each of them will enrich the relational life of the couple without interfering with their decisions and with their affective world. On the other hand, highly conflicted couples, where there is an absence of mutual trust, will experience greater difficulty in maintaining common and shared friendships. Each partner maintains separate friendship groups, where friends tend to take sides. During couple therapy, a quick way to evaluate couple functioning is simply to ask the partners whether they have and share common friends. The very fact that friends become easily involved in the couple's difficulties and are often the "confidants" of one or the other partner makes them a valuable resource in therapy and it would be very useful to ask them to attend the session as consultants to the therapist. Their contribution will be fundamental in better understanding the frustrations, suffering and feelings of failure in each partner in a collaborative and non-judging context (Haber, 1994). In bringing friends in for a session, it is important to note that they are asked as intimate experts of the individual rather than about the couple's issues. Normally, the friends who really help are generally longstanding friends, people who have shared the common growth processes or aspects of family development of one or other of the partners. In this case, their attendance at a session will be enlightening, as it will highlight family events or relational difficulties that do not directly relate to the couple's present conflict, but help to understand better other affective dimensions.

A second, equally important parameter for understanding the social identity of each partner relates to his or her working life. In a society increasingly centred on double careers, it is common that each partner spends more time at work than at home. Relationships with work colleagues carry relevance not only on a strictly business level, but also assume functions of affective support and personal exchanges. In a harmonious couple, the respective work experiences can enrich their relationship and mutual understanding. In high-conflict couples, the work place can be regarded as a threat and an enemy to defend against. Not infrequently, in situations of poor vitality in the couple, the work environment can represent an opportunity for one or the other to develop emotional or sexual extra-marital relationships, which ultimately will further damage understanding and trust in the couple.

The birth of a child: a major transformation in a couple's relationship

The transition from being a couple to becoming a family is a very challenging stage that requires a shift at both cognitive and emotional levels. The passion and intimacy shared exclusively by two partners now has to open up to include a newcomer, the baby, who becomes a priority in terms of love and care. During this transition, the adults have to learn how to remain intimate and loyal to each other through the active presence of a third person. In this new triad, rules, roles and interpersonal space have to be redefined and transformed. Becoming parents also involves a shift in connection, responsibilities and roles within the families of origin, where the grandparents' functions and love for the child will need to be given room.

In a harmonious couple, the child does not represent a threat to the couple's intimacy and love. According to Johnson (2004), they developed a secure attachment bonding in their intimate relationship. They easily adapt to including a new dimension to their relationship and parenthood does not interfere with their couple alliance. On the contrary, it enriches their bond, and the affection and care for the child are shared and enjoyed by the extended family. Are we describing an ideal couple, too perfect to be real? Do we encounter these types of families in therapy? It is precisely because we have seen many couples like this in therapy that we are certain that we are not idealizing this type of family structure. These couples tend to access therapy when they are faced with sudden adversity or loss. Dramatic events are present in the life span of any couple or family all over the world. The significant difference in harmonious couples is that they have a healthy coping system and have access to a rich array of resources that they and their families can activate in situations of extreme pain and stress. I remember working with a couple where an adolescent son died suddenly while taking a shower because of a malfunction in the heating system, or another couple, where a child was born with only half a heart and the parents kept the child alive while he underwent a series of surgical intervention over a period of years. These are not heroic families; they are made up of couples and parents who are able to show an incredible level of energy and togetherness to deal with dramatic life conditions or with their grief, asking and receiving help from extended families, friends and professionals. On the other hand, many other couples do not know how to cope and join forces with their family of origin when faced with life-threatening situations and can easily split or disintegrate.

The professional runaway and the over-dependent wife

High-conflict couples come to us for couple therapy because they are in deep crisis because of competition, mutual misunderstanding and betrayal. However, often they are brought to therapy because of psychosomatic, behavioural or relational problems manifested by one of their children. In this second case, described in several publications (Andolfi, 1994, 2002; Andolfi & Mascellani, 2013; Andolfi, Falcucci, Mascellani, Santona & Sciamplicotti, 2007) as *camouflaged couple therapy,* the initial request is based on the children's symptoms while, in reality, the distortion is in the relationship of the high-conflict couple who are in a very unbalanced position in respect to their family of origin. A case in point follows.

A couple are worried about the conduct problems of their 13-year-old daughter in school and they look for help. Their marriage is in trouble: the husband, John, had a recent affair and is angry with the wife because she has been controlling his life since their teens, when they met at school. His wife, Carol, has been playing mother to him for over 20 years and she feels that "he never grew up". He is a well-known professional, but at home, he is always angry and isolated. John describes his recent affair as "a way to get out of the prison". When asked about his extended family, he said that he left home when he was a teenager and never reconnected with parents and siblings. He sees them occasionally but has no feelings for or attachment to them. Of course, they do not know anything about his present situation and the great crisis in the marriage. In contrast, he has been well accepted by his wife's family, and almost adopted by them. He states that he had no real mother but, paradoxically, ended up having two "foster mothers", his wife and his mother-in-law! His wife is always calm, wise and never loses control, but she does not acknowledge his affair as she views it as "an adolescent's way of acting out". They are both very lonely: John is a "professional runaway", and Carol learned very early in her own family to conform and keep quiet. She depended all the time on her mother's wise advice, and in her marriage has replicated this pattern with her husband. Their daughter, Rebecca, is caught in her parent's issues. She has taken on both roles – the role of wise, over-responsible young woman while, at the same time, she has inherited Dad's rebelliousness and discharges her tension at school through conduct problems.

The miracle of adoption

Unstable couples are bonded in a dysfunctional way by their mutual insecurity and loneliness. They are not able to imagine separating, but they are in constant search for reassurance. They often have a history of neglect or mental illness in the family of origin, as in the case of Steve and Jenny, married for 15 years. During the past eight years, Steve and Jenny had been struggling to conceive and tried *in vitro* fertilization several times without success. Finally, they succeeded in adopting a child from an Asian country. They came to therapy to get advice on how to bring up in their home country, Italy, a foreign child, Ray, who looks and act strangely and is developmentally very slow. From the onset of therapy, the couple gave a very strong definition of their marriage: "Our marriage has been dead for a long time and we only care about Ray". This little boy was at the centre of every thought and daily activity in the house. Jenny complained constantly that Steve spoilt Ray too much and bought him all the toys and electronic devices that he himself never had as a neglected child. Steve said that Jenny was too severe and detached, and that she displayed the same emotional situation she experienced during her childhood, with no closeness, no expression of affection, no attention from parents. The parents' interactions were based only on mutual criticism and complaint. Their attention and fears were totally centred on Ray. The boy was at risk of becoming very spoilt at home, and further damaged by his peer group at school, where he plays the role of the "clown" in order to get attention.

The assessment of the sibling relationship

Generally, siblings grow up, mature and grow old together. The sibling bond covers all phases of the family life cycle, and because of this, they are the witnesses to and active participants in all kinds of family events. In this respect, Minuchin (1974), defined the sibling relationship as the "keeper of the family frontier", stating that the relationship between siblings represents the first social laboratory where children can cement their relationships as peers. In this context, children support or isolate each other, accuse each other and learn from one another. In this world of peers, children learn to negotiate, to cooperate and to compete. Siblings are often neglected in therapy, especially when the medical model is favoured, which focuses mostly on individual symptoms and very little on family development. A relational assessment, on the other hand, can benefit from the presence of the sibling subsystem in joint family sessions, whether the client is a child or an adult. Their participation is an excellent opportunity to evaluate the permeability of family boundaries, the presence of positive or negative triangulations in the family's history, to explore generational alliances, early parentification or emotional disconnections, sometimes caused by family unfairness related to age, gender, physical differences and favouritism.

A very important element attesting to the quality of the relationship between siblings is what Bank and Kahn (1982) define as level of access. Belonging to the same gender and proximity in age determine high access. For example, when siblings play together, attend the same school, share the same friends and common life events, their relationship is characterized by reciprocity and empathy. The sharing of emotional experiences leads to an intimate and tight bond, qualified by a high degree of loyalty, which might be even deeper in situations of inadequate or dysfunctional parental presence (Dunn & Plomin, 1991). At the other extreme, siblings with low access often belong to opposite genders or have an age gap that does not allow for the sharing of family events. Sometimes, they do not live in the same house and they might act as if they belong to different generations. Low-access siblings can also be caused by children being divided, taking sides with one of the parents after a hostile divorce. Moreover, nowadays the growing number of step-families has caused an increase in siblings with a low level of access, with a large age gap between the children of the first marriage and the children of the new couple, and sometimes, because older siblings become envious of the newcomers. There are also cases of children who are close in age but who are incapable of collaborating and sharing life experiences, as well as siblings of widely different ages, where the eldest becomes a kind of hero for the youngest, a guide to follow in times of difficulties (Andolfi & Mascellani, 2013).

In short, the horizontal relationship between siblings, regardless of gender and age, depends greatly on how much the parents allow their children to become siblings, without triangulating them negatively and without involving them in their couple dynamics or in "family mandates", which sometimes undermine the natural generational alliance between siblings. Hypotheses on the family's functioning can be made from observing siblings in the same room, during a family session, by the way in which young children can play freely together or create distance, by refusing to participate in common activities. This is even truer of siblings who are teenagers, when we can observe their body language and the quality of interactions among themselves and with adults. Using a multi-generational model of intervention, adult siblings can be invited to a special consultation with the clients in therapy. It is amazing to see how early imprinting and the different roles played by siblings from childhood can be re-enacted many years later.

References

Andolfi, M. (1994). The Child as Consultant. In M. Andolfi & R. Haber (Eds.), *Please, Help Me With This Family*. New York: Brunner/Mazel, pp. 73–89.

Andolfi, M. (Ed.) (1999). *La Crisi della Coppia*. Milan: Raffaello Cortina.

Andolfi, M. (2002). Couple Therapy as a Transforming Process: Reflections on Couples' Stories. In F. W. Kaslow & R. F. Massey (Eds.), *Comprehensive Handbook of Psychotherapy*, Vol. 3. New York: Wiley, pp. 359–388.

Andolfi, M. & Mascellani, A. (2012). Psicopatologia della Coppia Contemporanea nell'Italia Contemporanea. In P. Donati (Ed.), *La Relazione di Coppia Oggi*. Trento: Erickson, pp. 181–215.

Andolfi, M. & Mascellani, A. (2013). *Teen Voices. Tales of Family Therapy*. San Diego: Wisdom Moon Publishing.

Andolfi, M., Falcucci, M., Mascellani, A., Santona, A. & Sciamplicotti, F. (Eds.) (2006). *La Terapia di Coppia in una Prospettiva Trigenerazionale*. Rome: A.P.F.

Andolfi, M., Falcucci, M., Mascellani, A., Santona, A. & Sciamplicotti, F. (Eds.) (2007). *Il Bambino come Risorsa nella Terapia Familiare*. Rome: A.P.F.

Bank, S. P. & Kahn, M. D. (1982). *The Sibling Bond*. New York: Basic Books.

Dunn, J. & Plomin, R. (1991). Why are Siblings so Different? The Significance of Differences in Sibling Experiences Within the Family. *Family Process*, 30(3), 271–283.

Haber, R. (1994) "With a Little Help From my Friends": Friends as Consultative Resources. In M. Andolfi & R. Haber (Eds.), *Please, Help Me With This Family*. New York: Brunner/Mazel, pp. 112–131.

Johnson, S. (2004) *The Practice of Emotionally Focused Couple Therapy. Creating Connection*, 2nd ed. New York: Brunner/Routledge.

Minuchin, S. (1972). Structural Family Therapy. In P. Kaplan P.J. (Ed.), *American Handbook of Psychiatry*, Vol. 2. New York: Basic Books, pp. 178–192.

Minuchin, S. (1974). *Families and Family Therapy*. Cambridge, MA: Harvard University Press.

Whitaker, C. A. (1989). *Midnight Musings of a Family Therapist*. New York: Norton.

6

THE CONSTRUCTION OF THE THERAPEUTIC STORY

The formation of a therapeutic alliance with the family

As stated in the first chapter, this model of therapeutic intervention with families in distress is experiential and the goal is to search for individual and relational resources by reframing pathology and looking at the positive connotations of people's difficulties. In individual therapy, the alliance is formed simply between the therapist–client dyad. This process is more complex when we have to build an alliance with the family as a group. When an individual client asks for help, she usually knows what she is looking for; she has a personal motivation and an idea of what to get from therapy. When a couple ask for help, we need firstly to understand whether one partner brought the other one to therapy, sometimes coercing the partner to attend therapy, or whether they have a shared motivation to attend. Then we need to understand the nature of the problem and their definition of it. Often, there are disagreements on many levels. It is not uncommon for couples to provide different answers to even the simplest questions. For example, in answer to: "How long have you been experiencing this difficulty in your relationship?" one partner might answer, "For the last six months", and the other might state, "For more than 15 years".

The situation is even more complex when we have two generations in the room, like two parents and a child who is presenting with some sort of psychological difficulty. One parent might push for therapy while the other is against it, or has come just to accompany the anxious partner. Alternatively, it might be that one enlists therapy to help the child, and the other has in mind to fix the marriage through the child's problem. Not to mention the possibility that the problematic child might totally disagree with the parents' idea of looking for help through psychotherapy, denying any need for personal help. So, how do we build an alliance with the entire family, which will transform competition or disagreement into collaboration with and trust in therapy? In addition, how, as therapists, do we avoid the risk of taking sides with one part of the family unit, which replicates what happens with children when they are triangulated and divided? We have been facing these very crucial questions for a number of years in our clinical practice. In the early years, we experienced and described attempts to protect the client from being scapegoated in the family in the rigid family interactions, by taking his place and becoming, ourselves, the temporary target of family projections (Andolfi, Angelo, Menghi & Nicolò-Corigliano, 1983). Learning from our mistakes and developing a better understanding of the use of a triadic model, we were able to build an alliance with each family member, together with a solid meta-alliance with the family as a group. Instead of positioning ourselves as the third side of the primary triangle, we learned how to move in and out of the interactions and become a relational link capable of activating different family triadic configurations over three-generational levels.

When the individuals are seen through their specific ways of interacting with their own tri-generational family, they appear as complex entities, full of contradictions and conflicts. For a therapist, however, these interactions become tools for understanding the internal world of each person when trying to grasp the implicit links between current behaviours and experiences and past feelings, which would otherwise be perceived as fragmentary and unrelated (Andolfi, Angelo & De Nichilo, 1989). The therapeutic relationship creates a dynamic movement between each person and the family as a whole, and between the past and the present. Therefore, we need to understand and take into equal consideration the reality presented by each member of the family. It is like being an expert "juggler" having three or more balls up in the air, with the self-confidence and skill not to lose any of the balls!

By being aware that it is impossible to enter into earlier family and individual experiences and transform past history, it becomes possible to construct a new story with the family. In a previous publication (Andolfi et al., 1989), we explained how to build a therapeutic story with the family in a special place that we called the *third planet*. The third planet provides a visual metaphor to describe an open space where family and therapist join, interact and discover new relational meanings for past family events and present problems, and share an enriching experience in order to activate change. The family members are expected to be active participants, as is the therapist, who is active, direct, creative and playful. We refer to a model of intervention based on mutual influence and emotional engagement, different from narrative family therapy, which has developed through social constructivism, where the therapist or facilitator keeps a more neutral position. In this, we are closer to Minuchin's position in answering the question: "Where is the family in narrative therapy?" (1998). In fact, in this article, he criticized the political assumption of social constructivism that the individual and the social environment are the main actors, while the family, as a mediator between the two, seems to disappear. For us, on the contrary, the family is the natural bridge between the individual and his needs and the larger social context. Without a doubt, the studies on the differentiation of self from the family of origin, the exploration of past family events and their connection to present issues have been a very important cornerstone for our further development as therapists. However, the most original part of our theory is the position of the problem child or adolescent in our schema of family intervention.

The child as co-therapist

As a direct learning from my many years of working with families, I have become disenchanted with the medical model and the main psychiatric orientation in dealing with children's problems. I do not deny the need to assess children's psychopathology, to provide individual treatment and prescribe medications to children with severe disabilities or the need to hospitalize them for short periods. What I consider damaging for the child, and limiting for the helping professionals, is to focus only on his sickness, reducing him to an object of investigation and, for this reason, depriving him of any personal and relational competence. The same feelings of incompetence and lack of direction are experienced by parents and extended-family members who become passive recipients of psychiatric and medical decisions. In many children's hospitals, it is common to observe medical professionals who meet with children privately, while the parents remain in the waiting room, passive and uninvolved in the proceedings. For years, I have been supervising professionals working in hospital settings, and I have always been struck by the lack of knowledge or interest many of them display in any topic that is outside of the patient's specific illness or dysfunction. Their discussions about the child are commonly centred on medical and treatment information. Sadly, many do not consider the relevance of knowing anything about the child's resources or assets outside of his symptoms and, even less so, any knowledge about the family's developmental history, nor do they give credit to parental opinions.

My greatest challenge in dealing with problematic children and adolescents has been to free them from the label of being the patient. At the same time, I have been very careful to avoid giving myself the label of expert and, for that reason, I work towards empowering parents for the sake of their children, as quickly as possible. The problem child as co-therapist or consultant has been discussed in several publications (Andolfi et al., 1989; Andolfi, 1994; Andolfi, Falcucci, Mascellani, Santona & Sciamplicotti, 2007; Andolfi & Mascellani, 2013). I have found that the best and quickest way to de-label the child is to transform her into a subject of competence from the very beginning of family sessions. My theoretical orientation is evidenced in the very first question I pose in session. Instead of asking: "What's the problem with your child?" or "How can I help you with your child?" I ask the child directly, "How can we [the therapist and the child] help your family today?" The child is often surprised and a usual response is: "I don't know. They [the parents] brought me here!" To which I reply: "Your problems brought your parents here, therefore we can explore how your problems can help your family". This way of reframing the problem and shifting the context of the encounter to a family exploration can have a number of advantages. It elicits curiosity in the child towards the therapist who is asking for his help and it might implicitly encourage collaboration from parents who see a therapist eager to look at their child's problem in a positive way.

The search for relational meaning in children's symptoms is a most creative and exciting therapeutic endeavour. Children's behaviours and facial and bodily expressions can be linked to some characteristic of the parents or to their relational patterns. For example, a child's encopresis can be reframed as the special "glue" to keep the parents together. An anorectic behaviour can become an extreme request for a mother's love. School phobia can become a protective device to protect a mother from the father's violence. A very angry face can be a "scream" to get the parents' attention. A depressed child can be asked whether he got his sad eyes from Mum or Dad. The symptom of bedwetting can be reframed as a crying penis, a bizarre metaphor to connect a child's behaviour to the father's total inability to cry and show vulnerability. The child and her symptoms are a special bridge to enter into the family in order to identify the nodal points in family development, as well as to explore the quality of inter-personal relationships and the presence of inter-generational distortions and to look for resources and hope. Drawing the family genogram together, using play as a communicational language in therapy and asking relational questions are active tools to create an alliance with the family as a whole. This is essential to allow positive change in the child's presenting problem as well as in the family group.

Even when the presenting problem is related to a crisis in the couple's relationship, the physical or symbolic presence of children in the session can help to establish a better alliance with the couple. Children are witnesses to adult relationships from the moment they are born, and even before, if we consider that the formation of the primary triad begins during pregnancy. Over the course of their life, they have learnt a great deal about their parents and can inform the therapist about their knowledge of family life, if we give them voice in therapy. Often children's voices are ignored when their parents are in turmoil. Unfortunately, many therapists and child protection institutions collude with the parents in the idea that children are better off if they are not included in the family battlefield. Through experience, we have found that this protective exclusion of children is, in fact, based on prejudices and on the professionals' inability to elicit their genuine resources, to play with them and to learn from their simple and immediate language. If we are ready to listen to them and to respect their opinions, children will offer information, hope, sensitivity and a fervent desire to help the family. In order to develop this skill of listening to children's voices and looking for the positive in the family, it is imperative for the therapist to do a lot of work on his or her self.

The inner self of the therapist and self-disclosure

In the 1970s, I was supervised by Haley at the Child Guidance Clinic in Philadelphia, a prestigious family therapy centre directed by Minuchin. I liked the sharp and creative suggestions received in live supervision from this very well-known and respected supervisor. Details of this supervision are described in my first book, *Family Therapy: An Interactional Approach* (Andolfi, 1979). What I liked less, however, was Haley's assumption that whatever happens in the inner life of the therapist is irrelevant to therapeutic success. Of course, that was also the period of "problem-solving therapy", when ordeals and strategic prescriptions were more popular than emotional participation and empathy in therapy. During the time I was supervised by Haley, I was working with an Afro-American family consisting of a single mother and her children, Alex, an 11-year-old boy presenting with secondary encopresis, and his two younger siblings. During those sessions, I was able to recognize how much of my inner self was activated. In fact, the solution to his psychosomatic disorder was not the result of ordeals or behavioural modification; rather, it was a direct consequence of his search for his missing father. I still vividly remember sitting with the boy in the clinic cafeteria, discussing how he could find his father, who had disappeared from this family's life several years earlier. Alex presented with regressive behaviours, but his mind was extremely mature and his motivation very strong. After getting permission from his mother, Alex began his independent search for his father in the truck stations in south Philadelphia, because his father had been a truck driver in the past. Alex eventually found him and the father came with him to one session, full of guilt and shame, but he had the courage to come and reconnect and, "magically", the encopresis symptoms disappeared! This might be called an indirect intervention, but I see many children who transform their dysfunctions, during therapy, when something more important to their personal and family life is achieved. Personally, I was very moved by this little boy and his search for his father during a time in my life when I was struggling to become a father myself. My alliance with this boy was coupled with a sharpening of my self-awareness. In fact, the recognition of something of my own inner drive to be a father, in the therapeutic process, had a powerful impact on Alex's decision.

Whitaker and Simons wrote a beautiful paper on "The Inner Life of the Consultant" (1994), in which they talked about *context shadows,* described as fragments of the therapist's or client's past experiences that, once brought into the light of our awareness, cast their shadow upon what has been said and felt in the therapy. Whitaker reflected about his inner self, stating that he enacted the part that the family members represent in his family, presenting the *me* that is the family's father or grandfather or mother or teenager. He enacted his own internalization of each of those roles to begin the process of bringing healing reality into the consultation. The emotional responses of the therapist, therefore, are very relevant in the encounter with the family.

However, for a long time, systemic theories were unable to incorporate family feelings, and even less, the therapeutic emotional responses that we might call resonances, in their model of intervention (Andolfi, Angelo & De Nichilo, 1997). They made the same mistake as psychoanalysts, when they were unable to give adequate attention to the phenomenon of counter-transference. Whitaker was one of the first to describe family counter-transference in therapy. He used any kind of free association and "crazy ideas" (this is how he defined any fantasy or imagination that was coming up in therapy) to enter into the inner world of his clients, in order to highlight family distortions and create moments of deep connection with the family's pain and difficulties. His therapeutic goal was to move deeper and deeper into the inner world of his clients in order to reach what was unthinkable and to move then to what was unimaginable (Whitaker, 1975).

Whitaker, Satir and the followers of a symbolic-experiential approach all used self-disclosure as a way to share their inner selves with families and couples (Whitaker and Keith, 1981a; Johnson, 2004; Satir, Banmen, Gerber & Gomori, 2006). Of course, it is very important to know when and how it is appropriate for the therapist to share personal events, fragments of experiences from the past in his own family or brief descriptions of other families' treatment. Firstly, he needs to rid himself of his "professional mask" and play his therapeutic role using his full self and humanity. Sometimes, therapists are too busy listening to words and understanding content, and so run the risk of missing a central component of therapy, which is their own personal resonance in the therapeutic process. Once they shift from doing therapy to being therapists, it becomes much easier to feel themselves in the room, and to enjoy the freedom of joining with the flow of clients' emotions.

Therapists have to be very careful when dealing with deep family emotions such as pain, anger, grief and so on. The therapist might not be prepared to get in touch with the intensity of these feelings, risking an unconscious projection of parts of her own self in therapy. This is the reason why co-therapy and group work (a good example would be the presence of a reflective team) have always been recommended in family therapy. Through time and experience, it is possible for a mature therapist to create an internal supervisor, in order to observe herself on a meta-level, while interacting with one or other family member. It is the emotional baggage of intimate experiences, experienced with the family, which favours her personal growth and gives meaning to her professional role. Moreover, the moral strength acquired by going through human suffering gives the therapist a serenity, well described by Roustang (2004), that allows her to contact the depth of other people's pain, without carrying it personally.

The relational skills of the family therapist

Early in my career, for several years, I was a client in therapy with a new Freudian psychoanalyst, and candidate-in-training at the Karen Horney Psychoanalytic Institute of New York. I spent many hours on a couch with my psychoanalyst sitting behind me, making very few verbal interventions and sitting very still, only occasionally making slight movements. I do not want to reflect here on the usefulness of that personal experience for my growth. I just want to report how limiting and constrained the setting of many models of therapeutic intervention can be, but, at the same time, to reflect on what we can also learn from rigid structures that add to our own library of relational skills.

Attentive listening and self-reflection

One skill I developed was the patience to tolerate long pauses and emotionally intense moments of silence. Later in this book, I will describe the difficulty many active therapists experience in keeping silent. It is important to keep silent in order to give space for something very relevant to emerge from an emotional void in the session. I also developed the skill of being an attentive listener, paying full attention to the rare but significant comments by my psychoanalyst, but also to my own voice, and the pauses between one sentence and the next. This skill of listening to ourselves while we talk is an aspect of what we, in the systemic-relational field, might call self-reflection. However, the most important teaching, coming from many boring hours of therapy that produced no change whatsoever, has been my capacity to cope with and tolerate my own sense of impotence and personal failure. Personally experiencing both impotence and failure has allowed me to feel more benevolent and empathic with families in distress, who might be experiencing similar emotions in therapy. Over time, it transformed into a relevant therapeutic skill, invaluable for contrasting the feeling of grandiosity and omnipotence so well developed in our roles and careers as experts in people's issues. In my long journey as a family therapist, I have to say that whenever I felt stuck in a deep impasse with families but had the presence of mind to remain still, I was able to get in touch with and experience my feeling of uselessness, which in turn triggered the family to feel a sense of aliveness.

Joining

Joining is a key word in the toolbox of the family therapist. Its first description came from Minuchin in 1974, and ever since, has been used by family therapists as a way to welcome families and make everyone comfortable, especially at the start of the session when clients might feel very tense or anxious. In his latest book several decades later, Minuchin, Borda and Reiter (2013) reaffirmed the importance of this principle, stating that it is not a technique but, on the contrary, it is a state of mind made up of respect, empathy, curiosity and commitment towards recovery, which has to be present from the beginning to the end of therapy.

I have often described (Andolfi, 1979, 1994, 2009; Andolfi et al., 1983, 1989) my own ideas about joining, which include a number of the therapist's qualities mentioned by Minuchin. The main question for me has always been to understand the useful level to join people in order to produce change. Sometimes it is possible to join people in their hopes and positive expectations for their life and present situation. On other occasions, it will be more useful first to get in touch with their pain and the solid core of their disquiet and to stay there. Observing, from the very beginning, the ways in which each member takes a seat and interacts with the others, using curiosity and imagination in asking questions, getting closer or moving away from issues raised are all relational skills we can use in order to break down the family barrier and the pressure exerted by the presenting problem.

Joining is the first step in gaining trust from family members, who will double-check the realness of our interest, and competence in dealing with their issues. Families understand very quickly whether we really care about them. Their evaluation of our authenticity is based more on details like small gestures and eye contact than on academic, verbal descriptions of our therapeutic plans. Joining does not mean agreeing with what the family expects us to do. They will also trust us because of our capacity to be firm and offer solid containment and a coherent structure to help them to confront their issues. Whitaker would describe this phase as the "battle for the structure", meaning that the therapist has to be in charge of the quality of the therapeutic context. There is no doubt that we need to resist any attempt from family members to impose judgemental or discriminatory connotations towards others, or to dictate the priority of topics in the therapeutic agenda. Sometimes mothers or other family members jump on the description of the client's (child's or adolescent's) symptoms as soon as they sit down in the first meeting, as they are anxious for an immediate solution. Any attempt to enlarge the focus, or to engage the family, might be considered a waste of time and a distraction from the "real problem". Therefore, we have to offer a secure and safe base for positive transformation, without antagonizing parents, by opening new doors to elicit the collaboration of everyone in the family.

Sara and the antidepressants

I once spent an entire hour listening to a mother who showed me all the prescriptions for antidepressants taken by her daughter Sara, going into meticulous detail about her moods and negative behaviour over the span of ten years. At the end of the session, the mother felt very good, not only because I listened to her for a long period, but also because of my curiosity in looking with care at all the medical prescriptions without interrupting her. Her silent daughter was also impressed by my empathic connection with both the mother and herself. In fact, during the session I chose to sit next to Sara, trying to "step into her shoes", to feel her mood and share the silence with her. At the same time, while listening to the mother, I conveyed to her an implicit message of support by passing her the toy I had been holding in my hands. At the end of the session, I turned towards Sara and said: "Your mother has been telling us today how much she loves you; therefore I believe we are now ready to get to know you and your family better in the next session". The mother smiled, felt validated and relieved, and fully agreed to the proposal. Sara gave me back the toy, saying with gratitude and with an open smile, "Thank you!"

Being direct

Being direct is a real antidote to protectiveness and political correctness, both of which operate according to the relational scheme of hiding difficult realities or truths to people, most often children, who are considered fragile and vulnerable. These act as a kind of defence, to avoid the danger of facing conflicts and losses in affective relationship. Being direct implies the ability to be authentic and to go to the heart of the matter, without beating about the bush. It is a relational skill, which aims to relate to everyone with true curiosity and openness, by making clear our opinions and intuitions. It allows us to get in touch with our clients' conflicts and suffering without hesitation or prejudice (Andolfi & Mascellani, 2013). Being direct could result in a kind of therapeutic provocation, but it is very different from being directive, which implies a certain level of authoritarianism and imposition on other people's opinions. Concerning children, I often say that for them "A painful truth is better than a pretty lie!" Parents and therapists tend to prefer to lie about difficult truths and to keep secrets in order to protect children.

The story of the haemophilia

I remember the incredible courage of two parents who, during a session, were finally able to share how they found out that their two young boys were affected by haemophilia. They had been notified about the first child's illness just one day after his birth, and shared how they had reacted to the news. The father, seated with his oldest son in his lap, was visibly moved. He spoke of his incredible happiness at the birth of his first child, and how "the world seemed to fall down on him" the following day, when he was informed of the condition. The mother then shared: "I gave you one more day of happiness, but I knew about it from the very beginning". At that point, I encouraged the boy to acknowledge his father's courage and, even more, the respect he showed towards his children by sharing his deepest feelings with them. The child then put his head on his father's chest and kissed him! It is important to mention that, for a long time, both parents had been in denial that haemophilia was a serious medical condition, treating the children as if they had the flu. Being direct as a therapist, and gaining the trust of parents and children, gave the parents permission to shift from keeping an impossible lie to revealing their true feelings and accepting a difficult reality, in a context of mutual love and respect.

The mother's suicide

In another case, a father brought his two sons for a consultation regarding a minor school issue with one of them. During the intake phone conversation, I asked the father where the boy's mother was and the father, after a significant pause, informed me that the mother had committed suicide but that his children did not know this sad truth. In therapy, I intuitively moved more directly to the mother's mysterious death. The children gave a very vague answer, saying that their mother had died in hospital of some kind of illness four years earlier, but they had never asked the father for an explanation during the intervening years. I encouraged the father to speak with the children as two mature teenagers, not as two little boys.

He felt so reassured and safe that he was able to open up, describing in detail the circumstances of her suicide. At a certain point, I encouraged the father to move to sit between his two sons and to caress them openly. The children were finally hearing a very sad truth, which was healthier then remaining suspended in a limbo of secrecy.

Being direct is a very important therapeutic skill because it helps us to reassure and give people permission to open up on painful issues. Of course, family secrets cannot always be addressed so easily because of the lack of mutual trust among family members and with the therapist. To force people to disclose secrets or reveal lies can be damaging and abusive. Therapists must learn about the right timing and the therapeutic arena must be a safe place to permit family transformations. Therapists need to feel comfortable and centred within themselves in order to be authentic and direct.

Playfulness and humour

Playfulness and humour represent the most creative and personal means of engaging the family and the therapist in the therapeutic encounter. They are still little used by family therapists, who prefer, by far, an adult and serious model of communication. Perhaps the discomfort that the therapist encounters in being playful is related to her difficulty in moving from understanding emotional situations to representing them in the session. While the need to understand is based on a cognitive analysis of verbal data, playful representation has an element of make-believe that allows us to dramatize desires, fears and painful experiences through words and actions. In order to play, in contrast to observing play, it is necessary for the therapist to rediscover firstly the value of playing for herself and then to suggest it as a vehicle for inter-acting and searching for resources in therapy. This requires the therapist to learn to use herself and her own personal characteristics, such as gender, age and her way of laughing or speaking, in order to get closer or move away, according to the needs of the situation (Andolfi et al., 1989). If the therapist knows how to take on different parts and roles in the session, and moreover, if she knows how to move from one generational level to another, playing now the child, now the old sage, family members will be able to move out of stereotypical functions and become unblocked (Whitaker & Keith, 1981b).

Playing with words

Playing with words helps us to construct a metaphoric language that originates from images and paints pictures, and sometimes camouflages or transforms, deep moods, denied fears and conflicts, and dysfunctional relational patterns. Such a language, built on visual images, has a much longer and deeper period of permanence and cognitive resonance than a language based on abstract concepts or on verbal statements in session. The curiosity sparked by the language of images, kept purposely cryptic and incomplete, helps to tempt the individual and the whole family to participate in a therapeutic story belonging to all.

Playing with objects

If playing manifests better in action, we have to recognize acting as a valuable method of inquiry and knowledge in family therapy. In several publications (Andolfi, 1979; Andolfi et al., 1983, 1989; Andolfi & Mascellani, 2013), we stated that the use of metaphorical language and metaphorical objects is indeed based on our ability to play with our clients in order to create or discover relevant connections. Tangible objects are chosen by the therapist or by family members for their aptness to represent behaviours, relationships, interactive processes or rules of the family in treatment. These objects allow the therapist to play with what he observes, meaning by play the creative fantasy that stimulates him to produce new associative links. He offers them to the family, urging them, in turn, to participate by playing with their own associations. A little crown, a hat, a shoe, a pile of books, a ball, a tie, a little mask, a scarf, a doll, a plastic sword, a family drawing, a world map, an empty or high chair are all objects that can be used in the session, and transformed into relational links. They can change shape and meaning, depending on their contextual frame and the intensity with which they become attached to different people's functions and to specific sets of interactions. Several examples of metaphorical objects have been described in my books because of their profound impact on people's conflicts and fears. The alternation between the concrete and the abstract, between reality and metaphor, introduces uncertainty and probability into the therapeutic system, opening new doors for change as well as a sense of lightness and playfulness, because of the *as if* quality of the message substituting the *yes/no* logic of common language. A very convincing proof of the usefulness of metaphors, through language and objects, came from long-term research on the follow-up of family therapy reported in the book *La Terapia Narrata dalla Famiglia* (Andolfi, Angelo & D'Atena, 2001). Families giving feedback about what they remembered most from the therapeutic process three to five years later frequently answered that metaphorical objects, like the ones described above, had the most long-term effect.

Playing with toys

An easy way to engage children is to make use of toys in the therapy room. In addition, the therapist might offer his own objects to start a special conversation, which often allows for the inclusion of siblings and parents. At one level, it is very good to play with children and adults in session, in order to enjoy the mode of playing, especially when this is not a common experience in the house. Children might say, "They don't play with me: my dad is too busy at work or my mum is too busy in the house". Most of the time, playing becomes a relational language to initiate conversations on family issues such as worries about children's problems, or marital conflict, in a very powerful, yet relaxed way. A positive result of playing is that it helps to bypass adults' defences and rigid thinking patterns. Personally, I always go to a session with a little movable object in my hands, like a Slinky or any flexible object that I can manipulate with my hands. Besides, I use this as a way of withdrawing from the intensity of the session and providing an avenue for me to concentrate on my own inner thoughts about the family. In other situations (like the one described above with Sara), I like to pass it to a family member such as the problem child, the overinvolved mother or the detached father, to convey my empathy or to silence an overly involved participant.

The use of humour and laughter

Humour can be defined as the art of perceiving and enjoying what is absurd or amusing. Humour also has an integral relational function in that it is a way to deal with emotional conflicts or external stressors in a light-hearted manner. It also allows people to laugh at themselves and to take things less seriously. Humour in itself does not contain the notion of contempt or insult that is often found in derision or sarcasm. In psychotherapy several authors have described the usefulness of humour, for example, in reducing interpersonal tension (Schnarch, 1997), in developing resilience (Nisse, 2007), in deepening the therapeutic alliance (Gelkopf, 2011) and in challenging the internal frame of reference of the client, through provocation (Farrelly & Brandsma, 1974).

Humour and play have much in common. They both involve a kind of meta-communication that occurs, for example, in the fighting games between fathers and sons or between partners. Implicitly, participants know that the fight is not real; in the same moment that the aggression is played out, it facilitates a new sense of closeness. When we introduce a playful framework in a way that is accepted and enjoyed by the family, humour and laughter can transform inter-personal meanings and produce an internal redefinition of reality in the partici-pants. Humour and shared laughter provide a new playing field that gives people permission to play with their problems without feeling belittled or judged. It helps to remove mutual blaming in therapy and useless symmetrical escalations. If one is capable of plain talk and optimism, when facing even very serious prob-lems, laughing about them will produce a positive effect. Whitaker considered humour to be a kind of anaesthesia that needs to be administered before under-taking the intervention.

Laughter has manifold effects in therapy. It can be a powerful tool to external-ize problems and promote empathy. It allows for a sudden burst of tension, which helps to relax the stresses experienced during the therapeutic process. At other times, silence can follow the sudden bursts of laughter, and this can promote fresh self-reflection. Laughter may also cause a family member to shoot a desperate look at someone else, burst into tears or even leave the session. At other times, laughter can help to dislodge feelings of boredom and helplessness in the family, and rein-troduce a sense of hope. Only in a safe context can family resources be activated.

Therefore, in order to produce meaningful effects, both humour and laughter have to be used carefully and at the right moment.

Rituals and dramatization in family therapy

Family rituals, large or small, are the events that give family life texture and meaning. Daily rituals, holiday traditions and rites of passage mark our time, create unforgettable memories and define us culturally as individuals, family members and community participants. We believe that family therapy in which family members come together for therapy is, in itself, a ritual, and perhaps it is the same with any form of ritualized psychotherapeutic encounter. The frequency of meetings, the sitting arrangements, the use of space, the structure of dialogues and the prescribed roles played by family members and therapist are all elements that describe a ritualized context. Several authors (Selvini Palazzoli, Boscolo, Cecchin & Prata, 1978; Imber-Black, Roberts & Whiting, 1988; Andolfi et al., 1989) have described the use of specific rituals in family therapy. Different theoretical models outlined specific therapeutic rituals according to the different stages of the family's life cycle (such as weddings, funerals, births, remarriage and adoption), or around difficult family issues (such as alcoholism, sexual dysfunction, illness). Therapeutic rituals also incorporate multi-cultural aspects of people's lives, including the larger social context, for example, the work of narrative therapists like White and Epston (1989), or the network therapy approach by Barreto (2008) in Fortaleza, Brazil. The Milan group created very sophisticated rituals and prescriptions, initially prepared by the therapeutic team through their discussion of various hypotheses on family relational patterns, and later prescribed to families at the end of the session. Rituals in this form were directives given by the therapeutic team to engage the whole family in some activity that exaggerated or broke rules and family myths (Selvini Palazzoli et al., 1978). In my clinical work, I preferred to move from a cognitive model, like that of the Milan group, to a more experiential modality. As described in this book, the use of dramatization, family sculpting and metaphoric objects allows therapists to move from understanding abstract concepts to representing concretely in the session family conflicts, fears and losses.

I have become a doormat for my husband

The use of images is very common in the language of the family. It is up to the therapist to gather these images and transform them into dramatized actions. Let us explore the difference between the cheerless statement, "I have become a doormat for my husband", and its representation in the session. Making the image of a doormat come alive in the session encourages the couple to express the emotional meaning of that statement as best they can. The doormat becomes a nodal point that initially addresses the marital relationship and, in the construction of a therapeutic story, may be extended to other relationships, at other levels. The tendency to act like a doormat can be explored in other generations: "Where did you learn to do that?"; Who was the doormat in your own family?"; "Who was cleaning his/her shoes on the doormat?" The therapist can magnify the provocation by asking the wife to bring a real doormat to the session, choosing the one that best corresponds to the feelings she is discussing. This could be further externalized by saying, "It would be nice to see how your husband walks on the doormat". The amplification of the couple's relational patterns, through a very concrete action, introduces an element of playfulness, with a comic aspect to it, which might help them to move out of a dysfunctional complementary pattern to search for new, healthier ways to be together.

The ritual of divorce

I once had a consultation with a Danish family, with a 15-year-old son, Frank, who suffered from anorexia. The parents divorced a few years earlier and they came together because of the mother's concern for her child. This case has been extensively discussed in the book *Teen Voices* (Andolfi & Mascellani, 2013). As is frequently the case, the parents had physically separated, but had not been able to close their chapter as a married couple. Even after the husband had moved to a nearby country, the wife declared, "I'll never have a new man in my life". The husband also remained dependent on his ex-wife's advice on administrative matters, and even on his choice of new partners, and, she, apparently, enjoyed that role. The confusion from this lack of boundaries had severely affected their children's emotional development. The older sister played the part of the impossible rebellious child, and Frank remained the mother's little boy, filling the void of the husband role with his symptomatic behaviour. With Frank's help, we constructed the family genogram, which brought much information on the respective families of origin to light. This paved the way for a therapeutic ritual, in which the parents, facing each other, declared their intention to divorce, and cut all the confusing connections between them. At the same time, in order to facilitate Frank's progressive emancipation, the father had to declare his commitment to perform parental functions directly, without delegating everything to the mother.

It is amazing to see the incredible power and efficacy of family rituals, when mutual trust has been created among family members and with the therapist. Rituals can also be very helpful in cases where warring couples have reached, with the help of therapy, the point of reconciliation. A ritual of remarriage can be created in the session in order to formalize and celebrate their new alliance. Children, relatives and friends can all be invited to the therapeutic wedding, to toast their future life. Rituals can also be used to deal with sudden or dramatic losses as they recreate a context for grief and allows client to re-emerge from profound pain or fears. An example case follows below.

The ritual of the murdered brother

A father came to therapy because for a long time he had suffered nightmares and projected his deep fears on to his only adolescent daughter. He worried that she would die violently, either by accident or murder. He had been unable to sleep because of these terrible fantasies. An exploration of his family history revealed some traumatic events. When he was a small child, he had been told about a terrible murder at the time of his grandparents' generation. A more significant event, however, was related to his brother, who, more than 20 years previously, had been shot to death inside a local hospital. Because of this murder and of the legal complications that ensued, he was sent far away from his home town when he was a teenager by his parents in order to protect him. I proposed a special therapeutic ritual, to be performed in the presence of his beloved daughter, to help free him from these terrible fears. My client was asked to recollect the most terrible moments of his experience of his dead brother. In order to facilitate closure, he was directed to talk to his dead brother in his own words, to say his goodbyes and to ask permission to move on freely in his own life without the burden of his grief and to let go of his fears around his daughter's life. To facilitate this ritual, I asked a colleague to represent this man's dead brother, and directed him to lie down dead on the floor, in the therapy room.

It was incredible to see just how well my client entered into this experience. He imagined his brother at the morgue, newly deceased. He very tenderly caressed him, and started to talk about his experience of being siblings, recalling that the brother, the eldest, was their mother's favourite child. He also expressed the losses he experienced, first and foremost because of his dramatic death, and secondly because, immediately after that, he was sent far away from his parents' care and love. While he was going through this symbolic ritual of closure, his daughter, who was sitting next to me, shared this profound experience in silence. It is pleasing to note that after this ritual the father was able to put his fears to rest.

References

Andolfi, M. (1979). *Family Therapy: An Interactional Approach*. New York: Plenum Press.

Andolfi, M. (1994). The Child as the Consultant. In M. Andolfi & R. Haber (Eds.), *Please, Help Me With This Family*. New York: Brunner-Mazel, pp. 73–89.

Andolfi, M. (2009). Salvador Minuchin: Master of Life and Pioneer of Family Therapy and his Influence on Andolfi's Professional Development. *Human Systems: The Journal of Therapy, Consultation and Training*, 20(3), 5–18.

Andolfi, M. & Mascellani, A. (2013). *Teen Voices – Tales of Family Therapy*. San Diego: Wisdom Moon Publishing.

Andolfi, M., Angelo, C., Menghi, P. & Nicolò-Corigliano, A. M. (1983). *Behind the Family Mask: Therapeutic Change in Rigid Family Systems*. New York: Brunner/Mazel.

Andolfi, M., Angelo, C. & De Nichilo, M. (1989). *The Myth of Atlas: Families and the Therapeutic Story*. New York: Brunner/Mazel.

Andolfi, M., Angelo, C. & De Nichilo, M. (Eds.) (1997). *Sentimenti e Sistemi*. Milan: Raffaello Cortina.

Andolfi, M., Angelo, C. & D'Atena, P. (2001). *La Terapia Narrata dalla Famiglia*. Milan: Raffaello Cortina.

Andolfi, M., Falcucci, M., Mascellani, A., Santona, A. & Sciamplicotti, F. (Eds.) (2007). *Il Bambino come Risorsa nella Terapia Familiare*. Rome: A.P.F.

Barreto, A. (2008). Community Therapy: Building Webs of Solidarity. In M. Andolfi & L. Calderon de la Barca (Eds.), *The Oaxaca Book: Working with Marginalised Families and Communities*. Rome: A.P.F.

Farrelly, F. & Brandsma, J. (1974). *Provocative Therapy*. Capitola, CA: Metapublications.

Gelkopf, M. (2011). The Use of Humor in Serious Mental Illness: A Review. *Evidence-Based Complementary and Alternative Medicine*, 2011, article ID 342837.

Imber Black, E., Roberts, J. & Whiting J. R. (Eds.) (1988). *Rituals in Families and Family Therapy*. New York: Norton.

Johnson, S. M. (2004). *Practice of Emotionally Focused Couple Therapy. Creating Connection*, 2nd ed. New York: Brunner/Routledge.

Minuchin, S. (1974). *Families and Family Therapy*. Cambridge, MA: Harvard University Press.

Minuchin, S. (1998). Where is the Family in Narrative Therapy? *Journal of Marital and Family Therapy*, 24(4), 397–403.

Minuchin, S., Borda, C. & Reiter M. D. (2013). *The Craft of Family Therapy*. New York: Routledge.

Nisse, M. (2007). Humor, Haine Symbolique et Résilience. Du Bon Usage Thérapeutique des Mots Obscènes Chez les Victimes de Violences Sexuelles. *Cahiers Critiques de Thérapie Familial et de Pratiques de Réseaux*, 39, 93–101.

Roustang, F. (2004). Che Fare delle Proprie Sofferenze? *Terapia Familiare*, 76, 5–18.

Satir, V., Banmen, J., Gerber, J. & Gomori, M. (2006). *The Satir Model: Family Therapy and Beyond*. Palo Alto, CA: Science and Behaviour Books.

Schnarch, D. M. (1997). *Passionate Marriage, Love, Sex and Intimacy in Emotionally Committed Relationships*. New York: Norton.

Selvini Palazzoli, M., Boscolo, L., Cecchin, G. & Prata, G. (1978). *Paradox and Counter-Paradox: A New Model in the Therapy of the Family in Schizophrenic Transaction*. New York: Jason Aronson.

Whitaker, C. A. (1975). Psychotherapy of the Absurd: With a Special Emphasis on the Psychotherapy of Aggression. *Family Process*, 14, 1–16.

Whitaker, C. & Keith D. (1981a). Symbolic Experiential Family Therapy. In A. S. Gurman & D. P. Kniskern (Eds.), *Handbook of Family Therapy*. New York: Brunner/Mazel, pp. 187–225.

Whitaker, C. & Keith, D. (1981b). Play Therapy: A Paradigm for Work with Families. *Journal of Marital and Family Therapy*, 7(3), 243–254.

Whitaker, C. & Simons, J. (1994). The Inner Life of the Consultant. In M. Andolfi & R. Haber (Eds.), *Please, Help Me With This Family*. New York: Brunner/Mazel, 66–72.

White, M. & Epston, D. (1989). *Literate Means to Therapeutic Ends*. Adelaide, Australia: Dulwich Centre.

7

THE LANGUAGE OF THE
THERAPEUTIC ENCOUNTER

Human beings are distinguishable from the animal kingdom because of the faculty of speech. We speak either verbally or through body language, looks, postures and silence. In their formulation of Systems Theory, Watzlawick, Beavin and Jackson (1967) declared a cardinal concept, that it is impossible not to communicate in human interactions. Every behaviour, including silence, communicates something about a relationship. It is necessary to learn how to be fully attentive when we are working with families in therapy and to incorporate a thorough knowledge of both verbal and non-verbal communication. This is particularly true when we meet with families from different cultures, who have unfamiliar language, cultural and relational rules. In this situation, it is not sufficient to translate and listen only to the words. We also need to interpret all the non-verbal signals that convey essential values and appreciate the diversity inherent in differing cultures. A competent therapist, therefore, needs to learn how to listen to and value every expression of language, whether familiar or foreign. She will also need to become a translator of different languages within the family itself, giving space to the language of both genders, masculine and feminine, and to those belonging to the world of adults and the world of children and adolescents.

We saw, in previous chapters, how important it is for the therapist to understand children's symbolic and playful language, or the often eccentric and contradictory language of adolescence, not tuning in only to the adult channel. Compernolle (1992), in his work with children, noticed how family therapy suffers from adult-centricity, highlighting the difficulty that many therapists have in looking at reality through the children's eyes, by regarding the adult observational stance as the sole and universal measure of assessment. In addition, some therapists who are faced with problematic couples' interactions find it difficult to break free from the limitations imposed by their identification with their own gender, which prohibits them from getting in touch with the language and non-verbal expressions of clients of the opposite sex. In the next few chapters, we will explore the vast nature of therapeutic language, distinguishing between verbal and non-verbal signals and concluding with the communicative aspects of silence.

The foundations of the therapeutic dialogue

Since the time of Socrates, a conversation between two or more people has been considered a potent instrument of knowledge, especially in virtue of the fact that it allows us to draw different conclusions each time new elements emerge. In fact, with the awareness worthy of the best relational psychologist, Socrates did not consider that he had preconceived knowledge to impart to his disciples. On the contrary, he taught his disciples the importance of critical thinking and the need to clarify their own internal reasoning by using a *dialogic-dialectic* method.

From the very first session, the therapeutic encounter is based on the theoretical model and the context within which it takes place. Thus, a psychoanalytic session will be very different from a hospital assessment (designed to evaluate a psychiatric disturbance), and even more so, from a family therapy session. As in the teacher–disciple relationship of Socrates' times, every intervention must follow a method that is clearly defined in context. Systemic Theory was a revolutionary way of looking at family relationships, moving away from linear causality, which was based on the Medical Model search for cause and effect in psychopathology. Circular causality, in contrast, believed that knowledge was gained by assessing the differences in the information imparted through questions and answers and by analysing the complex system of meaning framing behaviour (Bateson, 1979).

As Bertrando and Toffanetti (2000a) stated, the use of circular questioning, designed to highlight the implicit differences in the various family members' ways of thinking, has been an important and innovative contribution by the Milan school, and further elaborated by Tomm (1988), with his reflexive questioning. Though non-verbal communication is considered essential, the centrality of verbal language influences the session and everything becomes centred on discourse. Questions, new questions, reformulations and rituals are created with precise attention to verbal details and the choice of words.

The Milan therapeutic approach, as affirmed by Bertrando and Toffanetti (2000b), is without a doubt the most "logocentric" of those formulated during those years and became the basis on which subsequent narrative (White & Epston, 1989; White, 2007), and conversational therapies developed (Keeney, 1982; Anderson & Goolishian, 1988; Anderson, 1997). The formulation of hypotheses was also developed within this orientation and, together with circular questioning and neutrality, was considered a cardinal directive for conducting a session, and was widely used by systemic therapists in subsequent decades (Selvini Palazzoli, Boscolo, Cecchin & Prata, 1980). Therapists were encouraged to formulate hypotheses based on information collected about the family, either in the initial assessment or during therapy sessions. The formulation of a hypothesis was the starting point for therapeutic investigation, the validity of which would be verified during the progression of the session. This process of hypothesis formulation included a pre-session with a therapeutic team, which represented a kind of "collective mind", whose task was to look for helpful meanings with which the therapists conducted therapy with the family. In fact, the family was definitely present in this preparatory phase, but only in an indirect way, through the reading of very detailed intake forms previously compiled by members of the family. Over the years, profound changes took place even within the most orthodox systemic schools. One notable example was the shift from the controversial concept of therapeutic neutrality to its complete opposite, that of therapeutic curiosity (Cecchin, Lane & Ray, 1992). The therapist's role, however, still remains predominantly anchored in "mind" over action, valuing cognitive over emotional data.

This multi-generational model of family therapy accepts the fundamental axioms of Systems Theory, but focuses more on the development of the family historically over several generations. In this model, working with the family means including the child or adolescent, both in our conceptualization of the family and in therapy. The description of therapeutic conversation as described by the followers of the Milan school is more relevant in a dialogue with adults, but it is less appropriate when dealing with the playful and symbolic language of children, or the eccentric and contradictory verbal expressions of adolescents. We prefer not to formulate plans and hypotheses before meeting with the family "behind their back," as Whitaker would say. Rather, we believe in the formation of a shared motivation by all members of the family during the first session. A shared motivation is developed when all family members feel that they can get something useful out of therapy for themselves individually, even if the request for help is initially focused on the symptomatic behaviour of one member of the family, or on the couple's crisis. The motivations of the referring system (general practitioner, hospital, school, family member or other clinicians) are respected and taken into consideration. However, it is important not to confuse this with the motivation of the family to attend therapy.

Engagement with members of the family begins before the first session. It is our custom to ask the family member requesting therapy to send written information describing the family composition and the reasons for requesting therapy, including details about the history and relevant events in the development of the family. Typically, mothers are the ones who seek help for their child or adolescent in trouble, and are generally the ones who supply the information. We find that this process of providing relevant information helps them to feel useful and competent. Also of interest is the information that is given or omitted. Generally, they report precious and objective information "written more with the heart than with the mind". During the course of therapy, the personal explanations and truths of other family members will need to be included. This phenomenon of "partial truth", which we can define as *multi-partiality*, is particularly evident in requests for couple therapy, where the level of personal involvement and possible conflict is more intense. For this reason, we ask for both members of the couple to provide information about their situation before the first session. This allows us to gather different and sometimes contrasting information from both partners.

Gathering and selection of information

When first meeting a family, we have to decide how to listen to and select the information about a particular problem, according to the model, the context and the therapy objective. Listening to and remembering all the content and the details supplied by one or other family member during a joint session are practically impossible and, in many ways, useless. Thus we face the problem of how and what to listen to and, obviously, how to ask questions.

The inverted funnel

Families often provide a mass of data on a specific issue, the sheer volume of which might be overwhelming. From this mass of information, the therapist's primary objective is to select relevant data to explore the relational aspects of the issue and the developmental history of the family, which might otherwise be blocked. The focus here is on quality, not quantity. We use the metaphor of the inverted funnel to describe the position of the therapist, who learns to select only the most relevant information, which passes through the narrowest part of the funnel, letting all else run out of the funnel.

The story of Edith

Let us look at a case. A family requested therapy because their adolescent daughter, Edith, was anorexic and had been hospitalized on several occasions. The whole family was obviously very worried about the situation. The parents, separated for a long time, described in detail Edith's behaviour at the table and all her rituals around food and I felt the danger of being overwhelmed and stuck. To circumvent this problem, I interjected with a seemingly unrelated question as to whether they had ever previously worried about their oldest son, Patrick. Immediately, the parents looked sad and started talking about the son's genetic pancreatic illness, which had affected both the mother and maternal grandfather, who had recently died of the condition. I used the inverted-funnel metaphor, to select and filter information about Patrick's illness and its inter-generational component, to blend with information relating to the sister's anorexia. This allowed me to uncover how the siblings were unconsciously in a competition for their parents' love and attention, through illness. The exploration of another serious illness in the family, which had not been mentioned by the family during the intake process, helped me to view Edith's anorexia in a completely different light. Instead of viewing it merely as a bizarre and regressive behaviour, it highlighted her need for parental attention, which had largely been centred on Patrick because of his illness. The reframing of Edith's anorexia as an extreme signal of her need to feel loved and cared for by her parents became an important step in her parents' awareness of her neglect and her need for their love and attention. It also allowed for the construction of a healthy alliance between the siblings, who had lived for years estranged from one another.

The therapeutic puzzle

I have often been asked to describe my thought processes in my work with families that often demonstrate an almost magical intuitive process. The answer is not simple, and I believe that it is based on my ability to hone in on what is missing, unsaid, in the family story and to create the link between the missing pieces of the puzzle to the problems experienced by the family. This new awareness has a transformative effect on the family. There exists, without doubt, a kind of therapeutic intuition similar to that of the hunter or the detective that, together with a healthy dose of curiosity, allows us to link apparently disconnected parts of a story. In the family just described, the ongoing suffering of every family member from the endless medical interventions common to the treatment of genetic illness, affecting several members of the family, led to the breakdown and eventual separation of the parental couple. The onset of a new illness, Edith's anorexia, increased the tension on an already stressed family system. The family experienced these two types of illness as separate entities. Patrick's genetic illness was easily understood and empathized with, as he did not have a choice in the matter. However, Edith's battle with anorexia and its play with life and death were less comprehensible and elicited less empathy because of the inherent element of choice in recovery. Making significant links between these two family dramas allowed for a transformation in the family and encouraged family strength and resources. Connecting the pieces of the puzzle enabled this family to feel that they can make it together. Edith and Patrick, once divided by illness, can experience a new alliance as siblings in health.

This is, in fact, the objective of multi-generational family therapy – a method that teaches therapists to view the family as a therapeutic puzzle, to learn to be curious about what is missing or unsaid, and to identify and connect the missing pieces. This helps to identify resources and to create transformations in the family, which will allow them to feel they can face life's challenges together. It replaces the sense of being lost and alone with the feeling of strength and unity. Ultimately, it is a matter of creating a bridge between disconnected parts to form a complete picture.

Reframing and relational statements

Reframing

Reframing has been a well-used relational tool in System Therapy. Reframing was initially understood as a predominantly verbal strategy that provided a new interpretation of the problems faced by the family. A symptom or behaviour, "reframed", changed meaning. Reframing has been used in different ways across the history of family therapy up to recent times (Elkaim, 1990; Cade, 1992; Flaskas, 1992;

Sluzki, 1992; Sprenkle, Davis & Lebow, 2009; Fourie, 2010). It profoundly inspired Erickson's work on hypnosis (Erickson, Rossi & Rossi, 1976) and the Strategic Therapy of Haley (1976). It influenced the positive connotation of the Milan group (Selvini Palazzoli, Boscolo, Cecchin & Prata, 1978) and the shift from problem to resource of Brief Focused Therapy (De Shazer, 1985). Reframing was relevant in the Narrative Therapy approach of White and Epston (1989), moving from the problem to the person, through the externalization of symptoms. In addition, Keeney's original method (1983), in its description of the therapeutic conversation as a "visit to the museum", is based on a redefinition of the presenting problem.

I personally published a long article on redefinition in family therapy (Andolfi, 1979), in which I described three forms of reframing: firstly, within the therapeutic relationship; secondly, within the context; and thirdly, within the presenting problem. Despite the passing of time and the evolution of therapy, the idea that reframing goes beyond a strategy designed to change symptomatic or dysfunctional behaviour has remained consistent.

The *redefinition of the therapeutic relationship* is a dynamic process based on shifting the frame of reference from individual symptoms to issues in the family. It represents a challenge to the medical/psychiatric model that focuses on treating patients' diseases. Therapists need to believe in this philosophy of help in order to propose this model of intervention, and its efficacy needs to be accepted by the family in order for therapy to be productive. It changes the whole goal of therapy.

The *redefinition of the context* is based on the capacity of the therapist to transform the emotional and cognitive climate of a session in order for each family member to develop a sense of trust in the therapist and to feel empowered and pro-active in the therapeutic process. There are many examples of unproductive context. A context of waiting is one in which families are largely passive and wait for a solution from "the experts", much like that in a medical context, when clients wait to be prescribed appropriate medication for their particular symptomatology. In a judging context, the therapy room is turned into a tribunal, where one family member is judged by the others, or even by the therapist. A hopeless context is one in which family members present with a deep sense of despair. Without the creation of a positive and collaborative context, it is very hard to develop a productive therapeutic relationship. In the wrong context, even the best intentions of the therapist and the family can be frustrated.

Lastly, the *redefinition of the problem* is pivotal to the entire therapeutic process. Numerous problems, such as enuresis, encopresis, phobias, depression and anorexia, can be reframed from individual symptoms to relational indicators in order to promote transformations in the family. They can often be linked to the affective or behavioural attitudes of a family member, or to the dramatic or painful events that marked the developmental history of the family.

This art of reframing has been inspired by the work of Keeney (1983), particularly by his original way of conducting a therapeutic conversation by changing the "frame" of one or more words in a sentence. For example, Keeney states that, by decomposing the phrase "exploration of the parents' history" into three key words, we could, for instance, take the word "exploration" and move it to another context. By doing so, we would no longer be exploring the parents' history but, perhaps, be exploring the animal world and, in so doing, we would change the entire meaning of the sentence and of the conversational content. Later in this chapter, we will discuss the case of Vincent, brought to therapy by his mother who is worried because the boy "locks his door so he can play on his computer". In this phrase many different words could be moved around, and, as we will see in the dialogue that follows, the therapist chooses to move the level and meaning of the words "locks his door", thus redefining the problem and the objective of therapy. In fact, other locked doors will be explored, that of the maternal grandmother, when Vincent's mother was a child and, currently, "the mother's locked door" that prevents Vincent from seeing his father.

Relational statements

Relational statements are those assumptions which arise from the therapist's intuitive understanding of the relational dynamics in a family which form the basis of subsequent questions. These statements do not originate from explicit knowledge or information, but rather reflect perceptions that originate from observing family interactions during the session. A case example follows.

"For how many years have you tried . . . "

A 16-year-old girl is depressed and cuts her arms. The parents are separated, but continue to involve their two children in their arguments. I address the girl, who is sitting between the parents, visibly discouraged: "For how many years have you tried, in every way you can, to tell your parents that it is time for peace?" The girl, astonished by the question, reflectively repeats: "How long I've been trying?" To which I reply: "How many years . . . ?" The girl, in the tone of someone who feels understood and supported says: "three . . . , three years!" The implicit statement, in this case, is: "I understand how often and in what way you have tried to put an end to the war between your parents but I feel how difficult it is to achieve peace". It is at this point that the creation of a therapeutic alliance begins, allowing for subsequent interventions that touch directly on her behaviour and its redefinition as a relational signal: "When you cut yourself, is this for her [Mum], or him [Dad]?" Again, immediately after: "What needs to happen to stop this war game?" The girl replies with renewed energy: "They should start to communicate, to ask me how I am and not speak only about my diagnosis, my problems, but just about me, about my feelings".

Olga's smile

Sometimes a statement is based on an *implicit* assumption, as in the example just mentioned, but in other situations, it can represent a relational nodal point, an emotional junction on which therapists can reflect and construct other connections. During a session attended by her husband and parents, Olga describes the deep reasons for her sadness. Suddenly, following a humorous comment by the therapist, she allows a radiant smile, like that of a child, and almost identical to her mother's. I enquired: "Olga, who did you inherit that beautiful smile from?", and then, turning to the mother and looking directly at her: "Exactly the same eyes, the same smile!" I follow this with a more explicit statement: "For too many years that smile has been covered by sadness; now Olga is no longer free to smile and when she tries her smile turns to tears. Isn't that so?" "Yes, that's how it is", states Olga, feeling deeply understood. This is followed by a period of silence in the session. These statements demonstrate the relational aspects of Olga's sadness. Her repressed smile and her sadness belong to her, just as they do to the most significant people in her life.

Relational questions

In our therapeutic model, asking questions that connect are as important as listening to answers. Using a triadic lens is important when meeting with families, and questions should include at least three relational sides. From time to time, and depending on circumstances, the therapist can represent the third side of the triangle. The therapist may also observe family triangles that might include members of the same generation, such as spouses or siblings, or of two different generations, such as parents and children, or even three, if we connect a grandparent with a parent and child.

Individual questions

The relatedness of questions is very dependent on our therapeutic ability and flexibility, so as "to see connections" even when they appear to be absent. At times of particularly intense emotions, it is possible to ask a visibly sad person: "How do you feel at this moment?" From the tone of voice, the body language and the manner of eye contact, the client can perceive feelings of empathy and concern. At the same time, the non-verbal responses of other family members to both the question and answer can be observed. In this way, the therapist is able to glean significant relational aspects, even when the question is directed at a particular individual.

Triadic questions

Before describing the various forms of relational questions, it is important to clarify the basic structure of a triadic question. Let us imagine that a wife is suffering from depression and the therapist wants to explore its relational dimensions in session. The therapist might ask the wife: "What does your husband do when you feel so depressed?" In this way, the therapist places herself as the third element of the triad, acting as the observer of verbal and analogical exchanges between the couple, with regard to both the question and to the answer. Alternatively, the therapist might again ask the wife: "When you feel really depressed, what happens between your husband and your daughter?" Thus, the therapist can observe the family triangle from the outside and can perceive the affective links between father and daughter, in relation to the wife's depression. From the wife's answer, the therapist can expand his understanding of the relational models between the three when faced with an illness presented by one member of the family. It is easy to understand that, starting from a particular point, in this case the wife's depression, relational questions and answers can include other members of the family. These are the building blocks in the construction of the therapeutic puzzle.

Direct and indirect questions

Direct questions are questions we ask one member about another family member, or about their relationship. For example: "Do you feel disconnected from your wife?" In this, the husband can reflect on the distance he has placed between himself and his wife, and, more generally, on the quality of their relationship. Indirect questions are questions that ask individuals to put themselves in another's shoes and to report on this reflection. Enlarging on the example before: "Are you aware that you are never there for your wife and that this makes her feel sad?" Imagining how the wife may feel in an emotionally distant relationship initiated by him creates an affective intensity that helps to identify with his wife's lived experience of the relationship that might change his point of view. Indirect questions are useful in working with conflicted relationships, as people tend to be entrenched in their own definition of the relationship with little capacity to "enter into the heart and mind" of the other. Asking a parent to put himself in his adolescent's or child's shoes, and reflect on the child's emotions, can create a relational opening and dissolve the rigidity of his own point of view. "If you could speak for him, how would you describe your son's anger at feeling he doesn't have a father?" We might ask the son to do the same about the father: "If you were your father, how would you deal with a child who wants to run away?"

Comparison questions

Comparison questions invite reflections on "before and after" and "more or less" situations, as a way of gathering precious information on the life cycle of our client and on their relational changes through time. For example, comparison questions can be used to explore feelings of exclusion or social isolation, such as asking a person whether this feeling was present before leaving her country, or before the marital separation, or after a child left home, or after the death of a beloved parent. Furthermore, we can observe and understand the affective reactions of family members concerning both questions and answers. Comparison questions are also used to explore different aspects of the self as well as relational dimensions. By creatively deconstructing and then comparing the parts or relational options, we can elicit responses that highlight certain aspects of the client's personality or a couple's or family's complex relational ties.

For example, a man states that he feels worthless and cannot think of a reason to continue living. The therapist could ask which part of him is already dead and which is still alive – his head, heart, body or breath – and then look for the differences in his responses that can be used to help him regain hope in a life where he can feel of some value to himself and others. The apparent absurdity of deconstructing a person into separate components can be a stimulus for him to develop a curiosity in comparing different parts of himself. He might reply that his head is still alive, otherwise, he would already have committed suicide, but that his heart has died, as he feels broken-hearted. Other family members can intervene, providing emotional responses and useful suggestions in the search for something of value.

A doctor 24 hours a day

A wife described, in an irritated voice, her husband's childish behaviour and emotional unavailability at home, because he "is a doctor 24 hours a day". I asked: "Which part of him did you marry most, the child or the white coat?" The wife replied: "At the start I was fascinated by the white coat, but I later realized that I was left with the child, because the adult is always at the hospital taking care of others". These questions compared two relational qualities of the husband, according to her point of view. The wife's answers, both verbal and analogical, are useful in the construction of the therapeutic puzzle and pave the way to begin the exploration of the husband's perspective.

Hypothetical and metaphoric questions

These two categories of questions invite us to shift away from a predominantly logical way of thinking in order to stimulate more imagination and creativity.

Hypothetical questions

As if questions are hypothetical questions, that are a common part of daily life. Their use in therapy is manifold. Therapists need to adapt this "as if" language to the specific circumstances, to the themes we want to investigate and to the relationships we wish to explore. Examples of "as if" questions follow. When dealing with loss or absence a therapist could ask: "If your mother was still alive, what would she tell me that might help your family?" "If your father was able to listen to you, would you be interested in meeting with him?" "If your son was attending this session, where would he sit, on the side or between you two?" When looking for an alliance: "If your brother showed you more affection, what might change in your relationship?" "If you could open your eyes, would you be able to feel your wife's pain?" To discover other ways of relating: "If you learnt to play with your child, would you feel more competent as a father?" "If you could turn off the TV when you eat dinner together, what might happen?" "If your son was here, what would he do to stop you fighting?"

Metaphorical questions

Constructing metaphors is one of the best ways to strengthen a therapeutic alliance with the family. The family often provides metaphorical images to the session, and the therapist can appropriate them and suggest new relational meanings. At other times, the therapist offers an image that represents the family's intricate relational bonds. Whitaker called this way of working the *process of metaphorization,* to highlight its characteristics of connection and sharing. A few examples of metaphors that exist in the language of families follow and the therapeutic use of metaphors in a clinical setting will be described later in this book.

"I feel like a caged bird"; "My children have been wrapped up in cotton wool"; "I feel like a doormat, trampled on by all"; "He built a wall between us"; "I feel as empty as a squeezed lemon"; "He treats the house like a hotel, coming and going as he pleases." The language of images allows a special meeting between feelings, relational difficulties and concrete objects to take place: the cage, the cotton wool, the doormat, the wall, the lemon and the hotel can become important pieces of the therapeutic puzzle in our search for transformation in the quality of family relationships.

The locked door

A mother brought Vincent, her 16-year-old-son, to therapy because he always locked himself in his room to play on the computer. The parents had been divorced for some years and Vincent had no contact with his father, because he did not want to upset his mother.

Therapist (T):	"So, the reason you have brought your son to therapy is because his door is always locked?"
Mother (M):	"Yes, I don't think it's normal that when he's at home he locks himself in his room."
T:	"What is it that's not normal? That he locks his room because he's sad or because he doesn't want to speak to you?" (comparison question)
M:	"Because he wants to play with his computer."
T:	"When you were a child, did anyone in your family lock their door?" (inter-generational question)
M:	"Yes, it was often my mother, and I really hated that."
T:	"So, you don't like people who lock their door?"
M:	"No, no."
T:	"But in fact it is really *you* who locks the biggest door!" (relational statement)
M:	"I don't understand. Could you please explain?"

T	(addressing the son): "Would you like to explain it to mum?"
Vincent:	"As I don't feel I can go to my father's, that is the door you have locked."
M:	"Yes, that's true."
T:	"But what is it that stops you opening the door of your house and going to see your father?"
Vincent:	"Because she doesn't like him."
T:	"I know many wives who don't like their husbands, but their children use their legs and go and see their fathers, spend time with them and enjoy their company. But if you are locked in your room, how can you knock on his door?"
Vincent:	"Yes, that's how it is."
T:	"Was he really such a bad father?"
Vincent:	"Not with me, but with my mother, yes!"
T:	"So, if your mother told you, 'I have no problem if you want to see him', would you like to see him?"
Vincent:	"Yes, I would like that very much!"

After this session, many doors were opened!

Inter-generational questions

This multi-generational model uses temporal jumps as a therapeutic intervention to gain a better understanding of the family. Using current problems as a starting point, questions are designed to explore the inter-generational aspects of family relationships. As in the example just cited of Vincent's locked door (the current problem), we can shift the focus to other locked doors; that of the mother inter-rupting the connection between father and son. A generational jump is made by asking the mother to "become a child again", and remember who locked doors in her family. It then becomes easy to find connections (the therapeutic puzzle) between her experience of her own mother's locked door, as a child, and her new-found awareness that she is now the one locking significant doors.

In our adult lives we tend to replicate the same emotional climate as the one we grew up in. These precocious learning experiences can become relational scripts that are unconsciously repeated during other life stages, and within different con-texts and generations. It is precisely the recollection of an unpleasant past experi-ence Vincent's mother had with her own mother, during therapy and in front of her son, that gave her the courage to give her son permission to see his father, without feeling abandoned or betrayed. Not only does this free her from relational models learnt as a child, but it also has the effect of emotionally connecting mother and son through renewed mutual trust.

In another example, asking a child who has problems with aggression and con-duct disorder to speak about his father at his age, and to imagine his behaviour at home and his relationship with his own parents allows a shift in focus from the present situation to the parent–child relationship of previous generations. This temporal jump can provide unforeseen information, always rich in emotive connections. The son's imaginings of his father in his childhood are made up from his knowledge of family anecdotes and "half-truths" collected over time, and invoke the father's curiosity in hearing his childhood recounted by his child.

Another use of temporal jumps in the exploration of different generations' relational ways of intervening in response to the same psychosomatic signal can be seen in the following example. A ten-year-old girl's headache can shift to the mother's experience of migraines at the same age and in turn to the grandmother's migraines at a similar age, thereby exposing how stress is managed in the female line of the family. From this, it is apparent that the more generations that can be included in a question, the richer the answers will be, both on the level of awareness of family plots and of the most significant affective bonds.

James and Mia

With regard to couples in crisis requesting therapy, it is useful to connect personal and relational information of each partner to scripts in their respective family of origin, rather than focusing solely on the couple's domain, where we run the risk of information imparted in therapy being used as weapons of defence or attack. From the start of therapy, it was obvious that James' relational models were at odds with Mia's. He described her as a schoolteacher who was always ready to impose her knowledge. She, in turn, was exhausted by his childishness and incessant way of talking that resolved nothing. In fact, during the session, both partners played out patterns of behaviour so well described by the other. The wife displayed expert opinions on every subject and proffered advice on all matters. The husband spoke without reason, only to fill the silence. Each partner knew the other's fragility and limitations, but instead of helping each other, they judged each other critically and used this information as weapons in their interactions with each other.

I was able to bypass the couple's problems, and explored, individually, from whom in her family the wife had learnt "to be a teacher" and from whom in his family the husband had learnt to speak meaninglessly. Exploring the intergenerational components of a couple's problematic interactions helps to shift the discussion level. With the help of inter-generational questions, feelings experienced as children are relived. Mia had learnt and replicated, in the couple relationship, the part of schoolteacher played by her mother for many years when she was a child that she really could not stand. James remembered how, when he was a child, his father concealed any emotion behind words and that, even though the father was a cardiologist, he could "never feel his heart"! This journey into the past presented significant emotional exposure for both partners who were thus able to reflect on their internal world and finally feel some empathy and benevolence towards the other. They were able to appreciate that fragilities and defences against insecurities are a part of life, that, once emerged, can be accepted, without the need for conflict.

References

Anderson, H. (1997). *Conversation, Language and Therapy*. New York: Basic Books.

Anderson, H. & Goolishian, H. A. (1988). Human Systems as Linguistic Systems: Preliminary and Evolving Ideas about the Implications for Clinical Theory. *Family Process*, 27(4), 371–393.

Andolfi, M. (1979). Redefinition in Family Therapy. *The American Journal of Family Therapy*, 7(1), 5–15.

Bateson, G. (1979). *Mind and Nature: A Necessary Unity*. New York: Dutton.

Bertrando, P. & Toffanetti, D. (2000a). Sull'Ipotesi. Teoria e Clinica del Processo di Ipotizzazione. *Terapia Familiare*, 62, 43–68.

Bertrando, P. & Toffanetti, D. (2000b). *Storia della Terapia Familiare*. Milan: Raffaello Cortina.

Cade, B. (1992). A Response by Any Other . . . *Journal of Family Therapy*, 14, 163–169.

Cecchin, G., Lane, G. & Ray, W. L. (1992). *Irreverence, a Strategy for Therapists' Survival*. London: Karnac Books.

Compernolle, T. (1992). "Adultocentrism", unpublished paper presented at the Conference *Changing Families in a Changing Society*. Brussels.

De Shazer, S. (1985). *Keys to Solution in Brief Therapy*. New York: Norton.

Elkaim, M. (1990). *If You Love Me, Do Not Love Me*. New York: Basic Books.

Erickson, M. H., Rossi, E. L. & Rossi, S. I. (1976). *Hypnotic Realities: The Induction of Clinical Hypnosis and Forms of Indirect Suggest*. New York: Irvington.

Flaskas, C. (1992). A Reframe by Other Name: On the Process of Reframing in Strategic, Milan and Analytic Therapy. *Journal of Family Therapy*, 14, 145–161.

Fourie, D. P. (2010). Asking About Ambivalence: A Different Kind of Therapist Neutrality. *American Journal of Family Therapy*, 38(5), 374–382.

Haley, J. (1976). *Problem-Solving Therapy*. San Francisco: Jossey-Bass.

Keeney, B. P. (1982). *What is an Epistemology of Family Therapy?* New York: Brunner/Mazel.

Keeney, B. P. (1983). *The Esthetics of Change*. New York: Guilford Press.

Selvini Palazzoli, M., Boscolo, L., Cecchin, G. & Prata, G. (1978). *Paradox and Counter Paradox: A New Model in the Therapy of the Family in Schizophrenic Transactions*. New York: Jason Aronson.

Selvini Palazzoli, M., Boscolo, L., Cecchin, G. & Prata, G. (1980). Hypothesizing, Circularity, Neutrality: Three Guidelines for the Conduction of the Session. *Family Process*, 19(1), 3–12.

Sluzki, C. (1992). Transformations: a Blueprint for Narrative Changes in Therapy. *Family Process*, 31(3), 217–230.

Sprenkle, D. H., Davis, S. D. & Lebow, J. (2009). *Common Factors in Couple and Family Therapy: The Overlooked Foundation for Effective Practice*. New York: Guilford Press.

Tomm, K. (1988). Intending to Ask Lineal, Circular, Strategic or Reflexive Questions? *Family Process*, 27, 1–15.

Watzlawick, P., Beavin, J. H. & Jackson, D. D. (1967). *Pragmatic of Human Communication. A Study of Interactional Patterns, Pathologies, and Paradoxes*. New York: Norton.

White, M. (2007). *Maps of Narrative Practice*. Adelaide, Australia: Dulwich Centre.

White, M. & Epston, D. (1989). *Literate Means to Therapeutic Ends*. Adelaide, Australia: Dulwich Centre.

8

BODY LANGUAGE IN FAMILY THERAPY

Language, as explored in the preceding chapter, is based not only on what we explicitly verbalize but, even more importantly, on what we express without words. This implicit level of communication is provided by body language which is made up of all those non-verbal signals (mimicry, posture, movements, facial expressions) that are the foundation of kinesics together with the paralinguistic system, characterized by tone, voice frequency and rhythm and, lastly, by silence. Non-verbal communication is also based on proxemics that analyse how space is occupied in terms of greater or lesser physical distance, and the relational boundaries and multiple messages transmitted through physical contact. All these signals assume a relevant affective and cognitive value. We speak with our body, looks, posture, intonation and pauses between words. Things are communicated by non-verbal expressions much more frequently during our early development than in adulthood. Even though body language is a more spontaneous and universal way of communicating, as it is less bound by rules than verbal language, there is no general theory of non-verbal behaviour. In spite of increasing research in this field, we are still a long way from integrating it into a coherent body of knowledge. In sum, there are no grammatical rules we can learn from, but rather, it is a language to be interpreted, and as such, it is subject to ambiguity and can create a lack of understanding on a cultural level.

Birdwhistell (1970), Scheflen (1972, 1974) and Kendon (1994), the pioneers of kinesics, worked out a series of concepts and terms that refer to everyday actions (for example, behaviour at the table, around the home, greetings, kisses and birthday celebrations). The work of these authors revealed the enormous variety of experiences that are observable in spontaneous interactions, and the social and cultural nature of these non-verbal expressions. It also highlighted the importance of movement and action that, in those days, was obscured by the psychodynamic interest in the significance of language. As Scheflen described in *Body Language and the Social Order*

(1972), there are two schools of thought regarding the meaning attributed to body language. The first school of thought is based on a psychodynamic matrix, and tends to regard kinaesthetic behaviour as an expression of individual emotions connected to personal experiences. The second school of thought is based on an anthropological and ethological perspective, which proposed that posture, movement, mimicry and physical contact should be viewed in relation to a cultural context and social processes such as cohesion and group regulation. Working with families has led to an integration of these two diverging points of view. In fact, families express an entire range of verbal and analogical language, and allow us to observe what pertains to the internal world of each individual, as well as what is communicated and experienced in family interactions and, furthermore, to take into consideration the socio-cultural components that influence family interactions.

Eye language and facial expressions

Eye contact is the most powerful way of transmitting our intimate emotions of joy, fear, sadness, attraction, trust or anger and, at the same time, of signalling a multiplicity of needs and relational requests. It is human behaviour *par excellence,* characterized by complex cognitive and neurophysiological processes that induce a mental reworking of our body image, a kind of *visual empathy* by which we see through the eyes of the other, who becomes a mirror of our body (Baltazar et al., 2014). Perhaps the profound contact and emotional involvement experienced in important relationships (such as the gaze between a mother and newborn child or between two people in love) have led us to call the eyes "the window to the soul". It is important to note that eye contact has a very different meaning in Western and Eastern societies, and in any case, is strongly influenced by traditional and cultural aspects. Eye contact is one of the most relevant facial expressions in terms of body language. In fact, as Borg (2009) states, the ability of the face to convey information about us is second only to that of the eyes. The eyes, in fact, fulfil a number of functions at a non-verbal level. This ranges from expressing sympathy or empathy, and conveying the status of a relationship (we tend to stare longer at those we like), to exercising control, regulating interactions and signalling the alternation of roles between the speaker and the listener. From the manner in which we look at others and the way we are looked at, we can understand a great deal about the character of a person, about her fragility and defences. Extroverts, for example, use their eyes more frequently, and tend to be perceived as being more competent, likeable and socially more skilled, as opposed to the more introverted among us who tend to avoid other people's gaze and are, thus, perceived as less affable (Argyle, 2013). Furthermore, through the eyes we can convey positive emotions such as joy or surprise or, conversely, negative emotions like anger, anxiety or shame. Even the pupil plays an important part in eye contact; it can dilate or shrink according to the nature of the interaction and the relationship.

Besides eye contact, the overall facial expression includes a series of other signals imparted by the mouth, the eyebrows and the facial muscles. They are signals that allow us to express and recognize the fundamental emotions of happiness and joy through the smile, those of sadness through tears and the wrinkling of the brow, or those of anger and fear through strong tension in the facial muscles and eyes. The quality of face-to-face interactions is an important indicator in understanding the development of human relationships and of inter-subjectivity, starting from the observation of a newborn. The expression on the mother's face, and the active responses from the newborn baby looking for her gaze, have been the foundation of Tronick's (1989) research on the emotive regulation and inter-subjectivity in the development of the personality, through his famous experiments on the *still face* (expressionless face). In addition, Stern's fundamental work on affective attunement has been very relevant to demonstrate a mother's ability to adapt her behaviour to the baby's vital expressions (Stern, 2010). Ekman, Friesen and colleagues explored the dynamics of facial expressions in various studies (Ekman & Friesen, 1982; Ekman, Friesen & O'Sullivan, 1988; Ekman, Friesen & Davidson, 1990). They worked out a coding system based on anatomy, the *Facial Action Coding System*, taking into consideration their temporal timing, like in a photographic sequence. They were thus able to demonstrate that a forced smile can be distinguishable from a spontaneous one, based on its dynamic properties, that is to say, its duration, initial, apex and final timing. Cook (1973) refers to the existence of facial stereotypes, or shared identification rules, through which the outward appearance is related to the personality. There are, therefore, certain traits (such as roundness or thinness of the face, the presence of a beard or glasses) that orient the evaluation of subjects in relation to a sense of humour, intelligence or other personality qualities. The most communicative elements of an individual reside, therefore, in her physical aspect and manner of dress, and it is those actions and attitudes we detect in a person (appearance, poses and way of speaking) that induce us to define her personality (which we might consider pleasant, strong, depressing). Thus, character is assumed from the fundamental attitude with which the individual confronts life (Lowen, 1978).

Gestures and body signals

According to Ekman and Friesen (1972), gestures can be indicators of an emotive state. For example, a clenched fist can signal anger or arms raised high are indicative of a successful outcome. Gestures can also have a communicative value, such as the gesture of a child pointing with an extended index finger at an object he wants, or that of an adult who, also with an extended finger, can send a strong commanding or disapproving signal. In other cases, we can observe in conversation unconscious adaptive gestures, such as twisting a lock of hair around a finger or playing with a pen. Iconographic gestures demonstrate what we want to communicate visually, such as indicating the size of a child with the hand, widening the arms to show perplexity or placing the index finger on the lips to request silence. Feelings and emotions are further expressed and communicated by the way in which people occupy space with the posture of their body, by the way they move their trunk or walk, the way they stand or sit, lean or bend. Therefore, the orientation of the body, and the way we place it in space in relation to other people, are significant indicators of intimacy and collaboration, or conversely, can signal hierarchical, authoritative or highly conflicted relationships.

The experts in non-verbal language (Birdwhistell, 1970; Ekman & Friesen, 1972; Scheflen, 1974; Desmond & Morris, 1977; Lowen, 1978; Tronick, 1989; Fivaz-Depeursinge & Corboz-Warnery, 1999; Stern, 2010; Argyle, 2013) have described in detail a whole series of postural modalities that correspond to various ways of relating or communicating about the self. Scheflen (1972), in particular, described certain body positions that can help us to understand how emotive closeness or distance has been developed within the family. An inclusive position is characterized by greater physical proximity between two people, and together with messages conveyed through eye contact, to the exclusion of a third person, who is thus made to feel marginalized and more detached in relation to the other two. These processes of hyper-inclusion/exclusion are particularly important in relation to the study of the primary triangle and are extensively observed in our clinical experience with families. They also form the basis of interesting clinical research, such as that conducted by Fivaz-Depeursinge and Corboz-Warnery (1999), on verbal language and the communicative processes between parents and child, using Lausanne Triadic Play.

Body spacing and relational boundaries

Proxemics is a discipline that studies the way in which people occupy space according to the inter-personal contexts they find themselves. As such, physical proximity of a couple or members of a family will be different from that determined by a school or work context and, even more so, by a public context, such as a railway station or public square. The analysis of spatial context can provide much information about the feelings between people and the relationships of trust and power that exist between them. Hall (1966), an expert in proxemics, correlated spatial dimension to distance/proximity in human interactions, distinguishing four categories, codified by precise rules, and distances that vary in a very significant way within ethnic groups that are culturally or historically different.

Intimate distance implies a high degree of affective involvement, with more restricted access, where generally, members of a nuclear family, and naturally, the two partners in a couple, are accepted. This proximity presupposes physical contact, such as that between mother and child or two lovers. *Personal distance* relates to the space of close relationships (which can still include physical contact, such as an extended hand), but that admits more distant family members, friends and colleagues. *Social distance* is defined as the relational area in which we carry out all the activities that involve interactions with people we don't know well or at all, such as in business or professional meetings. At this distance, it is possible visually to assess the speaker's body, which allows us to understand better his intentions and control communication. *Public distance* is the distance appropriate to formal situations where no direct interpersonal relationship is established, such as a meeting, conference or university lecture, with considerable distance between speaker and listener, characterized by strong asymmetry between participants. Expanding on Hall's categories, Sommer (1969) lingered on the subjective perception of space, especially in relation to personal space. He described it as a kind of protective bubble where others are not permitted to enter. The invasion of this space will be perceived as an unpleasant intrusion of the boundaries people have erected around themselves. Therefore, we are talking about a boundary that delineates a space that varies from person to person and that reflects gender and cultural differences.

Physical contact

Physical contact takes place through the skin, our body's largest sense organ, which communicates to the brain our experience of the outside world, starting from the newborn, who through tactile experience receives the initial information from his mother and begins exploring the reality around him. The skin is therefore a fundamental organ not only in the development of physical functions, but also in terms of behavioural and relational cues. The primary way in which we relate to other human beings and the environment is, in fact, by touch. Touching and making physical contact are essential sensory factors, diffused throughout every part of the skin, in determining the structure of our world and the quality of familial and social relationships. Even though touching is not an emotion *per se*, its sensory elements induce neural, glandular, muscular and mental changes, which combine to form emotions.

There exist two types of physical contact. The first is contact with others signifying a particular relationship. It can range from more formal aspects codified within the family and culture of origin (such as a handshake, a bow, a kiss on the cheek as a form of greeting among friends, relatives or colleagues) to more casual forms (such as a hug, a slap on the back or giving someone a "high five"). The second type of physical contact is the contact with our own self. Self-contact consists of small gestures of touching various parts of our own body that can be repeated, especially in times of inter-personal tension, in an unconscious search for comfort and reassurance.

The paralinguistic system and silence

The vocal non-verbal system indicates the range of sounds emitted in verbal communication, independently of verbal meaning. It is primarily characterized by the *tone of voice*, which is influenced by physiological factors such as age, gender and the social and cultural context we belong to. In certain cultures, it is normal to speak in a loud voice; in others, the same phenomenon may be considered a lack of respect. The variation in tone of voice can be conditioned by a disparity in social level, or can represent a different way of transmitting our emotional state when faced with an extraordinary event. In this case, another factor can come into play.

The frequency of the voice can be lowered or raised, according to the context and hierarchy of the relationship.

The *rhythm of voice* can confer more or less authority to the spoken words. Speaking at a slow pace, inserting pauses between one phrase and the next, gives a solemn tone to what is being said, as, for example, in the context of a university lecture or a political speech. On the other hand, speaking in a fast rhythm tends to convey less importance to the words, either because of the irrelevant content, such as gossip, or because of a particularly agitated state in the speaker. In analysing rhythm, it is crucial to consider the importance of pauses. Empty pauses represent the silence between one sentence and the next, while full pauses are typical inter-jections of sound, also inserted between one sentence and the next, such as *mmh* or *ahh,* that are devoid of verbal meaning, but are significant on the analogic level.

Silence is also part of the paralinguistic system and represents a non-verbal com-munication with very strong characteristics and very different meanings within familial and social relationships. In Western societies, for example, there is a pre-dominance of verbal expression, at times almost considered obligatory within affective relationships, while in the East, silence is privileged as a significant way of communicating. Obviously, silence needs to be understood in relation to context. The silence between two lovers has a very different meaning from that taking place between two people whose relationship is cold and distant, which is again different from silence in the face of grief or sudden loss. In the following chapter, silence as a communication modality in family therapy will be explored, as well as the com-petence and difficulties many therapists experience in remaining silent, in order to understand better their clients' pain and lived experiences.

How to use the eyes in family therapy

The previous chapter described how to listen to and select the most significant verbal content in the construction of a therapeutic relationship. This section will focus on the way that therapists can better understand eye contact in order to observe the mes-sages that the various family members send each other through analogic language, and the self-observation of the therapist. Just as there is no grammar to study the rules of non-verbal communication, it is equally true that universities and training institutions tend to privilege the teaching and comprehension of what is said in a session (thera-peutic conversation) over what we observe with our eyes. This has led to a general definition of psychotherapy as the *talking therapy*, or the therapy of words. However, schools with an experiential orientation give particular respect and attention to visual and physical contact, as well as movement in the therapeutic space. Furthermore, a therapist who places the child or adolescent at the centre of the therapeutic stage must learn and use playful language, and move from the chair to the floor.

Over the years, I have often been asked, in wonder: "How can you see those things while in session with the family?" I believe that part of the answer lies in my early experience of sensory deprivation in moving from my home country, Italy, where I had specialized in child psychiatry in Rome, to the United States, where I worked in social and community psychiatry in a family therapy service in New York. It is common knowledge that, when we lose one sense, the other senses become more activated to compensate for the loss. I had to compensate immediately for my insufficient understanding of the English language with a more pronounced use of my eyes, to observe family interactions, in often dramatic situations, rather than listening to verbal content. This eye-opening practice to observe the non-verbal dance of those clients in front of me has accompanied me throughout my personal and professional life, especially in foreign countries, and has become an essential resource in my therapeutic toolkit. Even when you work in your own country, a good therapist needs to develop this skill of "opening their eyes to observe" to understand fully family interactions. The therapist has to learn to have a discontinuous attention and fluctuating listening skills between what is said and what can be observed.

Lung language

Another vital point of observation is to notice what I have termed *lung language*, which is the language of the lungs given when someone sighs deeply or gasps or is visibly holding their breath. Lung language reveals an internal emotional shift in relation to what is being said or experienced in the session. Lung language is not always expressed by the person who is talking; it can also be expressed and observed in a family member who is watching, or it can be in response to a question posed by the therapist. On observing the lung language of family members in session, the therapist can ask the person who gives a big sigh, or who gasps audibly, to give voice to what she is experiencing or feels has been hitherto unsaid, and needs the space to be voiced and acknowledged.

Seating arrangements in family therapy

A child who always sits between two parents, or two siblings who sit apart with a parent between them, or an empty chair occupied by a handbag or other objects between a couple in therapy is not just accidental and can tell us something about the affective distance between people. Also telling is the care an adult son demonstrates in making the mother or father comfortable, with tender gestures, as if returning to an earlier family time when, as children, we responded with attention to the affectionate care of a parent. Long term unresolved sibling rivalry can become visible through the spatial relationships that now-adult brothers replay in session as soon as they sit down. Young people or adolescents can signal their greater or lesser motivation to attend therapy by the way in which they enter the room and the position they assume soon afterwards when seated, by flaunting their total lack of interest through their body language. A girl who attends a session with an absent air, who sits down and leafs through a women's magazine as though she was at the hairdresser's, is certainly telling us something about her motivation to participate and perhaps about how she is feeling obliged to attend the session. It is common for children who have been brought to therapy by their parents to act out the symptoms from the very start of the session. The depressed child often sits down, apart and mute with her head down, the hyperactive child often jumps from one place to the other and the violent child will throw defiant and fiery looks at the parents or directly at the therapist, whom he immediately considers complicit in the parental plots against him. Couples in crisis can immediately show, through their looks and posture, feelings of profound unease, abandonment or betrayal and their mutual desire, through body language, to form a coalition immediately with the therapist against the other.

The therapist will also have to choose where to sit at the beginning of a session, and this will depend on how comfortable she feels and on her theoretical reference models. An orthodox psychoanalyst will choose to sit in an armchair, behind the divan on which the patient sits; the doctor or psychiatrist will place a physical barrier between herself and the client, consisting of a desk on which boxes of medicines and scientific books are visible. Relational family therapists have adopted a general stance of maintaining a more open space, without barriers, between themselves and members of the family. At most, there might be a coffee table where objects are placed, such as a box of tissues (a concrete metaphor to communicate that you have the space to show emotions during the session). Without a doubt, a semi-circular arrangement without intervening barriers speaks of a less hierarchical encounter (such as that of the doctor/psychiatrist), where the meeting is more "between people than about people". The therapist must feel at ease and competent in an open, less guarded space, where people are able to shift around, from whatever initial position they assume in session in order to get closer to or further away from others, or where the therapist can ask certain family members to change position.

By contrast, Whitaker in his clinical work always sat slightly apart from the family group and rarely moved from this marginal position, considering it more appropriate to adopt the peripheral view of the wide-angle lens, instead of zooming in on particular family members. In fact, he considered that focusing on individual details would be distracting and might endanger the appropriate distance he needed to keep him from becoming embroiled in family dynamics. Although Whitaker would position himself physically apart from the family, he touched them deeply with his use of symbolic, often absurd language made up of metaphors, crazy ideas and free associations (Whitaker, 1975). Satir shared the same symbolic/experiential model, but, in contrast, used space in a much more active way. Satir looked for relationships of proximity, favouring physical contact in a warm and affectionate way (Satir, Banmen, Gerber & Gomori, 2006). In my clinical work, I have always chosen a central position with respect to family members, who sit in a semi-circle in front of me. From this initial position, I am free to move around or to encourage family members to shift position.

How to observe the way people look

In our clinical work, the language of the eyes is given a lot of weight. Therapists need to be vigilant in observing both people and their non-verbal language and messages, and need to make eye contact with family members in order to create an implicit dialogue with each of them, being very mindful not to exclude any-one from this type of implicit affective bond. The therapist's gaze must transmit empathy, curiosity, warmth and a sense of security, to indicate that any type of emotion manifested during the session can be accepted and contained. Obviously, if someone shows discomfort at direct eye contact, or makes an active show of avoidance, it would be useless to force that barrier. In these cases, it is more useful to observe their visual and gestural responses to those verbal interactions that regard them directly. Children who are very dependent and enmeshed with their mother are often unable to reply without first looking their mother in the eye, as if to "ask permission to speak". On the other hand, it might be that a mother may start to cry and, automatically, as if by induction, the daughter joins in with her own tears. It should be noted that the shedding of tears is not always an authentic expression of grief or sadness. Sometimes, tears are revealed as a false expression of suffering, and can often be a strategic instrument of control and coercion to manipulate those individuals who demonstrate fragility or are emotionally dependent, as in the enmeshed mother–child situation or in highly dysfunctional couple dynamics, where tears can easily become "weapons of attack or defence". Similarly, smiles are not always a demonstration of joy or happiness and can at times more closely resemble a defensive grimace than an authentic smile, hiding the real emotions that have been repressed. Ekman et al. (1988) observed that authentic facial expressions could be distinguished from false or simulated ones based on their *vital dynamics*.

The therapist may be witness to an infinite variety of looks between various members of the family or couple. Looks of understanding, love and tenderness can alternate with looks of refusal, contempt or provocation and even hatred. Alternatively, she might witness looks of profound pain and endless suffering or of total impotence in the face of life events. It is important for the therapist to develop the capacity to hold on to herself, that is to say, to retain her integrity and not allow herself to be influenced in one way or another by the quality and intensity of the looks exchanged by family members. For example, the therapist must accept a look full of hatred or tears without prejudice or personal involvement. Otherwise, it becomes difficult to make space for a positive redefinition and to facilitate change. Given the emotive load of many family therapy sessions, the therapist will need to develop strategies to disengage visually and maintain her integrity when she detects the risk of taking upon herself the excessive weight of family issues. Collectively with the family, she might encourage a pause in the current interactions, which helps to decrease tension, by suggesting a game or encouraging collective laughter or a moment of silence. Individually, she might concentrate her gaze on an object in her hands, to detach herself for a few moments from the intensity of the session and give space for the collection of thoughts and inner dialogue.

The movement in therapeutic space

We share with Stern (2004) the idea that action is the main road to knowledge, and we believe that movement during the course of family therapy sessions is essential both on the level of evaluating a particular pathology and to produce change within the individuals and the family as a whole. Bowen's (1978) metaphor of the therapist as the *coach* of the family team is very similar to our idea of the therapist as an active builder of family links. The family provides the bricks and, together with the therapist, they change the "shape of the house". In fact, the most transformative and curative aspect of therapy is the experience of the therapeutic relationship, constituted by the interaction of vital forms (Stern, 2010). According to Stern, the vital force is that quality that unites all living beings, a kind of global Gestalt that is generated by the experience of movement, force, tempo, space and intention about live events. Therefore, the therapist has to encourage the expression of vital forms, which every family member expresses through movement and the dynamics of discourse (the paralinguistics for understanding one another), rather than through the strict meaning of words. In so doing, he will immerse himself and become involved in the therapeutic experience, identifying with each family member through a deep, affective resonance that brings to light traces of experiences that have been lived globally in the past and preserved in each person's memory, as well as in the collective memory of the family.

Jade's tears

Jade, a university student in her second year of psychology, was referred by her treating psychiatrist to attend family therapy because of her depression and frequent bouts of crying that completely paralysed her parents, who were unable to contain her breakdowns at home. Even in session, Jade's tears had the effect of making the parents feel very inadequate and functioned as a strategy to concentrate all the attention on herself and her illness. Recognizing the significance of her tears, and relying on her presumed competence in psychology, I asked Jade to provide a short essay on the various types of adolescent tears, and to write on the whiteboard their different expressions and meanings. Jade accepted the task with great pleasure, since this request was coming from a university professor, which made her even more the centre of attention. While the young woman wrote and classified in detail the different types of tears pertaining to different situations, the parents and I listened with interest, as if attending a university lecture. The effect of the lesson did not take long to produce results: from this analysis of tears I began to build a therapeutic alliance with Jade, who had never before been treated as such a competent person, either in her family or in her psychiatric sessions. This exploration of Jade's tears allowed me to enter easily into the developmental history of the family, in order to understand tears and grief connected to the losses experienced by the family at other times yet still active in the present.

Concretizing in therapy and the pathways of memory

We can find new ways of highlighting important aspects of relationships by doing something concrete in the session. For example, family sculptures, therapeutic rituals or role-playing, described in preceding chapters, privilege the use of actions and movement in the therapeutic space, choosing a specific period of time and place when representing family relationships. In doing so, we activate a "memory pathway" that takes form through the body language of the family members involved in the sculpture, and through the expression in their eyes and the absence of words. Equally, we can ask the same person to create a "wish sculpture" to imagine their optimal, future family relationships, after the resolution of present difficulties. Even in this case, the sculpture will have to take into account past experiences. It is only by reviewing these traces and those of the most significant bonds, internalized during development, that they will be able to imagine how to represent, through movement, a future different from the present.

With regard to memory pathways, we can briefly review a case already described in the section about therapeutic rituals (Chapter 6). A father was able to free himself from having death fantasies about his adolescent daughter that had been tormenting him on a daily basis, after enacting a "ritual of a wake for his dead brother" who was assassinated 20 years earlier. Tracing back the memory of his lost brother, and giving words during the ritual to old feelings of admiration and envy (as the eldest son had been the mother's favourite) had the effect of freeing him from the feelings of immobility and fear that had accompanied him for many years. These feelings had been so strong and persistent that they invaded and congealed other spaces and relationships, such as the one with his daughter. The daughter, sitting near the therapist, witnessed the father's ritual in silence and was finally able to understand his nightmares and his fears, and to identify with his pain and, soon afterwards, to embrace him in a new way.

Movement in the formation of the therapeutic alliance

If it is true that empathy is fundamental to the therapeutic relationship, it is equally true that movement is vital in the creation of the therapeutic alliance, particularly with the client for whom therapy has been requested.

The therapist's active movements

The shifting of the gaze is in itself already a movement *towards* the client by the therapist. Moreover, the ability to move towards or away from, to sit on the floor, lean towards, move around the room, change seats, move objects or write on a whiteboard are part of the "physical and mental gymnastics" of the relational therapist. Even though these are generalizations, it is useful to mention some of the movements by the therapist, differing according to age, gender and the family's cultural background as well as, obviously, the specific situation. To engage a child, the therapist must enter into his personal space, look him in the eyes and play. To make contact with an adolescent, the therapist must avoid looking her in the eye, approaching her instead from the side and surprising her in the interaction, identifying with her body language first and only later with her feelings. An adult is generally more defended and cautious even when he appears willing to collaborate. He must be engaged through the children, the problems and family events. The older person is generally like the child, and even with her, we can play and flirt discreetly. Entering into her memories is like giving sweets to a child, as she generally enjoys feeling like an important part of the family story.

Obviously, attention to gender and culture is very important in the creation of a therapeutic alliance through movement. For a male therapist approaching an adolescent boy, a husband or father is much easier and immediate because there is an innate and, in many aspects, universal understanding of one's own gender. The same can be said of a female therapist concerning the feminine world where motherhood, the care of children and even the way "husbands are looked after" involve aspects that are profoundly rooted in female identity. We therefore must learn how to move during a session, being mindful of the limitations of our own gender and age, always asking ourselves what influences a certain action might have on a person of the opposite sex or who is much older than the therapist.

Concerning other cultures, we should maintain a curiosity that allows us to be accompanied into other worlds, into countries and traditions that are very different from our own and learn "in the field" the different cultural meanings of body language and movement. If we are motivated by the desire to understand other cultural dimensions and to identify with different ways of expressing and conveying values and emotions, transcultural work becomes fascinating. The creation of a therapeutic alliance is facilitated by the initial position of respectful curiosity ("the I don't know position"), together with the desire to be guided directly by the family ("I don't know, show me, tell me").

The family's active movements

Obviously, we should also encourage movement of family members among themselves as well as with us. This movement will reveal much about the greater or lesser flexibility within the couple or family. At times, the relational space seems frozen, or posture and movement seem blocked, because of open conflict or irresolvable pain. Bringing a couple, or father and adolescent child, physically closer at the very moment that a communication level has been opened between the two will serve to reinforce the beginning of a new understanding after a period of perhaps long and difficult emotional distance. Just as important is the creation of a space shared by the members of a family confronted by a recent loss, in order to feel the strength of being with each other instead of being divided by desperation and grief. In the next chapter, we will further discuss the usefulness of facilitating affective closeness through physical contact among family members.

In my clinical work, I choose to join with the family by engaging first with the problematic child or adolescent through a verbal reframing of his/her symptoms. The next step is often to ask the identified client to come and sit next to me. This request represents a way of evaluating, through an active movement, the child's or adolescent's readiness to trust my intentions. At the same time, this physical proximity increases a therapeutic alliance and is an implicit message for an active collaboration with the child that widens the therapeutic framework, and allows for exploring the family's history and events, with him/her as a precious guide. At other times, joining with family is a collective movement, as in the construction or completion of a family genogram. In this case, all family members can converge on the centre of the room, around a small table, where the genogram is to be drawn. It is very rare to get a refusal to take part in this family activity, because people are generally positive about the therapist's interest in knowing family details. This family map outlines inter-generational bonds, family events and specific ways of dealing with the adversity of life as well as with the happiest stages in family development.

Another useful activation of the family is when the therapist invites the family members to participate in the formulation of a therapeutic contract. Everybody, sitting around a table, is encouraged to contribute and to write down the main points, to accept what has been agreed upon, and to sign the contract, the therapist included. Making things concrete in therapy instead of merely talking is a conceptual shift of paradigm: from understanding with the head to doing with the hands, with gestures and physical closeness. This shift is useful when relational blockages or open hostility towards someone in the family are visible in the session, or when someone is dragged to therapy without any personal motivation.

The Algerian rock

I consulted with a family in Paris. Ali, the father, is described from the beginning as an impenetrable rock. During the consult, his wife and three adolescent daughters threw glances full of hate and resentment towards this man, who seemed immovable in his affective detachment. From information gathered prior to the consultation, I learnt that the family had emigrated from Algeria. After noticing everybody's looks of resentment towards Ali, I moved closer and sat next to him. I took a small world map out of my diary and gave him a pencil, asking: " Ali, can you show me where you were born, and where in Algeria you have emigrated from?" Ali looked me deeply in the eyes, surprised by an unexpected question and, feeling very moved, took the pencil from my hand. He spent a few long moments looking at that tiny map and then marked with a point "the exact place", a little village in the desert of Algeria (which was not depicted on the map), where he was born and grew up. The therapeutic challenge was either to stand in front of the rock, or to accompany this man back to Algeria in order to explore family issues and go beyond present anger and family resentment.

How to change the rules of the game

During a session with a couple in crisis, the two partners were involved in a tough competition to dismiss one another; each assertion by one was followed by a ferocious criticism by the other. It was like an endless competition in order to win the final game, but neither one was able to win because the result was always a draw.

Observing this exhausting game and realizing the couple's relational impasse, I went to the paperboard, divided a sheet into two parts, one side with his name and the other with hers. Then I continued listening to their "dialogue" and started marking the score: as soon as one scored a point, the other would disagree and it was a draw. At the end of the session, I took the sheet of paper, with all the scores; I tore it into small pieces and put them in a plastic bag. I instructed them to keep the bag in their bedroom as a memento of their current impossible relationship. They had to keep the bag for as long as it was needed, until "they were doing better", that is to say, until they were able to listen to and appreciate each other's reasons. Six months later, with the help of the therapy, they were able to "change the rules of the game" in their relationship, and they returned the plastic bag, with a smile of relief.

How to transform an Indian girl's refusal into collaboration

Shanti, a 14-year-old Indian girl, was sitting in the waiting room, refusing to take part in a family therapy consultation requested because of her eating disorder. The parents tried to convince her to join the session, but she responded with an obstinate refusal. The therapist also tried, but even this attempt was futile. Shanti's parents and younger sister were in the therapy room, waiting to know whether the session would take place. I decided to risk another refusal. The fact that she had come to the family therapy centre, even if only to remain in the waiting room, seemed to me an ambivalent, and therefore hopeful, signal. Prior to the session, I received some general information from their therapist. I learnt that the family migrated from Mumbai when the girls were very young and there had been a long history of conflict between the parents, and even disagreement about how to address the girl's problems. I went to the waiting room and saw Shanti, a very tiny girl looking more like a child than a 14-year-old adolescent. She was sitting still, gazing at the floor. I sat on the chair next to hers, looking straight ahead, not attempting even to turn and look at her. I introduced myself, giving her my full name, adding that I was from Rome. After a brief pause, I asked her, in a casual tone of voice: "Do you know where Rome is?" After a short pause, she responded in a feeble voice: "Yes". This seemed an encouraging response that allowed me to reply, in the tone of a curious traveller: "I went to India once, many years ago; I visited the south by bus, starting in Mumbai, going through Madras, travelling as far as Cape Comorin and coming back via Goa and Pune". At this point, the girl looked up at me with curiosity. I responded to her look with a smile, drew closer to her chair and said: "What do you think? Shall we go upstairs together and help your family?" The girl got up and followed me into the therapy room.

References

Argyle, M. (2013). *Bodily Communication*. London: Routledge.
Baltazar, M., Hazem, N., Vilarem, E., Beaucousin, V., Picq, J. L. & Conty, L. (2014). Eye Contact Elicits Bodily Self-Awareness in Human Adults. *Cognition*, 133, 120–127.

Birdwhistell, R. L. (1970). *Kinesics and Context. Essays on Body Motion Communication.* Philadelphia: University of Pennsylvania Press.

Borg, S. (2009). Language Teacher Cognition. In A. Burns & J. C. Richards (Eds.), *The Cambridge Guide to Second Language Teacher Education.* Cambridge, MA: Cambridge University Press, pp. 163–171.

Bowen, M. (1978). *Family Therapy in Clinical Practice.* New York: Jason Aronson.

Cook, M. (1973). *Interpersonal Perception.* New York: John Wiley.

Desmond, M. & Morris, J. D. (1977). *Man Watching: A Field Guide to Human Behavior.* New York: Abrams.

Ekman, P. & Friesen, W. V. (1972). Hand Movements. *Journal of Communication,* 22, 353–374.

Ekman, P. & Friesen, W. V. (1982). Felt, False and Miserable Smiles. *Journal of Nonverbal Behavior,* 6, 238–252.

Ekman, P., Friesen, W. V. & O'Sullivan, M. (1988). Smiles When Lying. *Journal of Personality and Social Psychology,* 54, 414–420.

Ekman, P., Friesen, W. V. & Davidson, R. J. (1990). The Duchenne Smile: Emotional Expression and Brain Physiology. *Journal of Personality and Social Psychology,* 58, 342–353.

Fivaz-Depeursinge, E. & Corboz-Warnery, A. (1999). *The Primary Triangle: A Developmental Systems View of Mothers, Fathers, Infants.* New York: Basic Books.

Hall, E. T. (1966). *The Hidden Dimension.* New York: Doubleday.

Kendon, A. (1994). Do Gestures Communicate? A Review. *Research on Language and Social Interaction,* 27, 175–200.

Lowen, A. (1978). *The Language of the Body.* New York: McMillan.

Satir, V., Banmen, J., Gerber, J & Gomori, M. (2006). *The Satir Model: Family Therapy and Beyond.* Palo Alto, CA: Science and Behaviour Books.

Scheflen, A. E. (1972). *Body Language and the Social Order.* Inglewood Cliffs, NJ: Prentice-Hall.

Scheflen, A. (1974). *How Behaviour Means.* New York: Anchor Books.

Sommer, R. (1969). *Personal Space.* Inglewood Cliffs, NJ: Prentice-Hall.

Stern, D. N. (2004). *The Present Moment in Psychotherapy and Everyday Life.* New York: Norton.

Stern, D. (2010). *Forms of Vitality: Exploring Dynamic Experience in Psychology, the Arts, Psychotherapy, and Development.* New York: Oxford University Press.

Tronick, E. Z. (1989). Emotions and Emotional Communications in Infants. *American Psychologist,* 44(2), 112–118.

Whitaker, C. A. (1975). Psychotherapy of the Absurd: With a Special Emphasis on the Psychotherapy of Aggression. *Family Process,* 14(1), 1–16.

9

SILENCE AND TOUCH

Two powerful ways to connect

In the preceding chapter, I referred to the general meaning of the paralinguistic system and of silence in the context of familial and social relationships. I would now like to investigate in more depth their communicative and transformational aspects within the therapeutic relationship.

Pauses of reflection

In therapy, spontaneous discourse and even the therapist's vocalizations are imbued with vital dynamics (Stern, 2010). The therapist is unable to open her mouth without affectively resonating with what has just been said or is about to be said by someone in the family. This means that even the slightest variation in tone of voice, in the pauses between one sentence and the next, and even inarticulate sounds like "uh uh" or "aa haa", emitted by the therapist, assume a different meaning and value according to the emotional context of the session. In particular, a pause in the conversation becomes vital in creating discontinuity and making room for *reflexive listening,* as Carl Rogers (1951), would say, on the part of both the therapist and those in the family who wish to attune themselves to the thoughts and emotions of the other family members. An accelerated rhythm in the therapist's verbal interjections is often indicative of her anxiety or embarrassment in stressful or conflicting situations, while maintaining a calm and slow pace allows for the creation of verbal voids that invite everyone to "remain present" instead of reacting emotionally to unpleasant communications.

Frequently, especially with couples in crisis, the partners' voices overlap because each wants to reiterate their own truth, immediately reacting to the other person's answers, which they find unacceptable. In this conversation, where interaction is replaced by reactivity, the therapist should avoid superimposing a third voice, her own, and should aim to become a music conductor rather than someone playing a different musical instrument. Furthermore, in situations of *symmetrical escalations*, the reciprocal nasty looks between the partners are a further provocation. The therapist should avoid the escalation of animosity during the session by creating a kind of visual barrier, to facilitate the alternating of answers to her questions so that each partner will, in turn, listen to and be listened to, without interruptions. This process has the effect of slowing down the rhythm of the conversation, and creates pauses for reflection that are useful in shifting on to the cognitive level and moving away from emotional over-involvement. When trying to reach the authentic feelings of a person it is not useful to remain at the level of "gut reactions". This was well understood by Bowen (1978), several decades ago, when he experimented in couple therapy and found that, in order to interrupt the circuit of reciprocal reactivity, it is more useful to avoid any one-to-one interaction and shift the conversation from the "What do you feel?" level to the more introspective one of "What do you think?" Reflecting on the issues and activating the "ears system" have the effect of lessening tension and bringing partners closer, because each will be able to hear the reasons of the other, and identify with the suffering and frustration of the other. When training psychotherapists, I have often advised them to record family therapy sessions and later to listen to the dialogues again, paying particular attention to the pauses between one spoken sentence and the next one. A greater number of pauses is indicative of a more effective therapeutic process, where a discontinuity rich in implicit meanings is created, favouring greater sharing and cooperation between family members. Listening to the therapeutic conversation is also a way of assessing the therapist's capacity to tolerate pauses and to enter into people's most profound experiences without feeling anxious about "having to do something" to fix it. Significantly, there are pauses by the therapist when faced with situations of grief, loss or grave illness that open the space to a warm silence, supportive of the family's pain.

The significance of silence of the family and of the therapist

Coming from years of psychoanalytic training, I remember with relative unease the long silences of my psychoanalyst who was waiting for me, as the client, to start speaking. Apart from the method, I have never understood why the analyst had to be mostly an active listening post and why they were trained to avoid taking any verbal initiative, such as introducing a topic for discussion. At the same time, I fondly remember warm silences that conveyed to me her presence to my pain in situations of loss and total bewilderment. These silences were much more important than words and helped me to feel a profound sense of connection, what Stern called "affective attunement". Those silences, made up of respect and profound emotional participation, have remained with me as a precious enrichment of my toolkit as a relational psychotherapist. I have transferred these skills from a dual context of one-to-one therapy to the more complex, and far more vital, multi-person family therapy context. Keeping silent during a session with a family has very different meanings and communicates different emotions to each member of the family. During my training as a family therapist, I never read an article, or heard a lecture, on the theme of silence in family therapy. Apart from what was said regarding "silence as a communication modality" by Watzlawick, Beavin and Jackson (1967), in the description of the axioms of the pragmatics of human communication, silence in therapy has been much neglected. Furthermore, the postmodern theories seem to reaffirm the primacy of conversation and verbal language in understanding the deep discomfort of couples and families.

The therapist's silence as a listening tool

The therapist's silence can have different functions during a session. There is the dynamic silence characterized by listening to the verbal interactions of various family members, and the silence that follows a question or statement by the therapist while waiting for a reply. A calm silence associated with expressive eye contact tends to convey a feeling of warmth and affective closeness. This encourages family members to make active interventions within a safe context, where people feel heard and understood. The therapist's silence thus becomes a kind of modelling that family members can adopt as a way of communicating during the session. It acts as an antidote to anxiety, which generally forces a faster speaking rhythm and frequent mutual interruptions. The therapist's calm and serene demeanour are contagious and can bring about order better than many words or prescribed behaviours.

It would not be appropriate to instruct a person who talks incessantly and interrupts others to keep quiet. It creates a judgemental context, in which the authority of the therapist must not be contradicted, and invokes possible resentment in the person who has been silenced. I would rather reframe the "excessive talking" as a special form of care to protect others from personal exposure. Alternatively, I would ask the same person who in his/her family of origin the "excessive talking" comes from and whom, in so doing, she is trying to protect. More simply, I might give her the object I often play with in my hands during the consultation, telling her gently that by playing with it she can distract herself and become more able to listen to others. In addition, giving her something of mine might encourage an implicit therapeutic alliance, thereby producing the "magic of silence".

Listening and speaking are two complementary modalities that facilitate interactions in the therapeutic space and unblock situations of relational impasse, such as the one between partners, or a parent and adolescent, exasperated because each is convinced of not being heard by the other. In addition, in situations of conflict, there is the risk that each person might continue to speak until he is finally heard or, on the contrary, may take refuge in a silence loaded with resentment. In the most enmeshed situations, I have often found that "playing with the problem" can be a very effective strategy. Therefore I can play with silence by giving my watch to a partner or to a parent or a child and giving them a time challenge by asking: "How long will you be able to listen to your partner [or child] without giving in to your impulse to intervene?" Generally, because it is a game, it is accepted without resistance. I then might propose a certain time of silence/listening that is not violated because it is part of the rules of the game. If the time challenge is honoured, I can congratulate the person who has overcome the often difficult challenge of keeping silent. At this point, I find family members are able to take turns more easily, as it is now more difficult to interrupt. The positive outcome of this intervention is that everyone will feel they have a voice, and together they can open their ears.

Silence as a support to family grief

Often, as therapists, we have been faced with a family's grief following a sudden death, a suicide, a devastating separation, a chronic illness, an episode of domestic violence, a psychotic breakdown, a natural disaster or a business failure. One of the first questions we ask ourselves is, "How do we deal with this pain?" followed by "What do we do with it?" There is no right reply to either question but, without doubt, each therapist has to find the most adequate answer according his competence and personal sensitivity. In dealing with people's pain it is important to be aware of the context within which the therapist operates (working in a hospital is very different from therapy in a private office), and of the specific requests of the clients in asking for help.

In the development of family therapy, much has been written on the theory of change, and around the most effective strategies to help families to transform. Sadly, much less has been written in regard to the therapist's skills to "stay with the suffering" brought by families in therapy. It is true that, when faced with the tragic loss of a child or a significant member, many families enact defensive strategies of denial and refuse to accept the event, because otherwise it would be too painful. The therapist can adopt similar defences too. Fearful of taking on excessive grief, many therapists find a way of staying out of family despair by using a number of justifications and rationalizations in order to remain in a safe zone. Other times, very "altruistic" therapists end up taking upon themselves the pain brought to therapy by the family as if "it was their own", stepping over the boundary between what concerns the family and what pertains to the therapist. Keeping silent, when faced with a family's grief, and staying with the family's suffering are two relational modalities that enable an affective attunement with that dimension of family grief. In this condition of silence, the therapist can put herself in the shoes of each parent concerning the loss of their child, and connect these imaginings to the non-verbal signals transmitted by various family members during a session.

The death of a child

The calm silence of the therapist is the best antidote to give containment to anguish and appease the cries of despair of a family facing the profound drama surrounding the death of a child. The Rosi family came to therapy a few weeks after the loss of Nico, their eldest son, aged 18, who died tragically at home due to a domestic accident (a malfunctioning gas boiler). Nico was at home alone at the time of his death, and the mother, coming home from the market, found him dead in the bath. The parents and younger brother, Giorgio, aged 14, abandoned their home the night of the accident and went to stay at the house of friends, because they could not cope with staying in the place where Nico had died. Their friends, who witnessed their despair, did not know how to help, and requested my intervention.

My initial sessions with them were full of silence and listening. I do not remember doing or saying anything other than following their stories – the mother's desperate cries, counteracted by the father's disquieting, uncomprehending silence, and the brother's disbelief. I listened to the detailed description of finding Nico dead in the bathroom, of their running away from home, of the mother's sense of guilt for going to the market, and the guilt of the father who, in spite of being an engineer, had not found the time to repair the faulty boiler. I looked carefully at the albums of photographs brought by the mother to show me how handsome, athletic and happy Nico was! I observed in silence how each of them dealt with their loss – the mother by going to the cemetery to see the son's grave twice a day, the father by shutting down into total silence, and Giorgio by speaking of his brother's loss only to his closest friends, embarrassed by his mother's desperate tears and feeling the father's absence and distance. They had become three islands and each reacted in their own way to an event that had suddenly disconnected them. They had been such a lovely, close, happy family, as the mother pointed out by showing me the photos of many trips taken together before the accident.

As I myself had experienced the tragic loss of a brother many years earlier, I remember how my silence was even warmer and more intense, marked by fragments of personal experiences that, instead of muddying the waters, helped me to attune better to the family's varied expressions of grief and loss. I am convinced that our clients are well aware of how we manage to stay with their deepest anguish and emotions and how we are able to contain them. They are able to differentiate between our silences – those of embarrassment and of flight from those of respect and real emotional participation. Time is an indispensable healer, but while it is true that time can allow for a transformative experience, it can instead be a dead time. The first condition is what Roustang (2014) calls the *oblivion that preserves*, within which change happens because life has not stopped and the poignant pain no longer invades our existence, but disappears into the deepest layers of our being. A dead time, on the contrary, is the *oblivion that obliterates* and does not allow us to accept that that tragic event really happened and that the family has been touched by it. In which case the loss of a child has taught nothing and changed nothing.

Several months after therapy began, the Rosi family were able to regain a sense of belonging and sharing and to overcome a long period of mutual distancing. The first change happened, as it so often does, through a "concrete action", which precipitated significant transformations. They had to decide whether the house, to which they had never returned, should be sold or renovated, in order to allow to them to return home. Having chosen the second option, our sessions shifted to discussing together plans for the renovation of the family home. They would show me drawings, sketches, ideas for internal restructuring as if I too "was going to live there". Thus, while my first silence had a containing function for their anguish, now my listening and affective participation were an answer to their invitation to share a new life project with them.

The acoustic mask

At times, the silence of an individual can assume pathological dimensions, as in *elective mutism*, where often a person cannot speak in order to cover, through her silence, the anguish and profound unease of other family members. Di Nicola wrote an article titled "The Acoustic Mask" (1985), that related to a consultation I had done in Toronto many years ago, where a 13-year-old girl had decided not to speak in the house by becoming totally mute. During the course of the session, I introduced a game that consisted in communicating with the girl via head gestures and written notes that we exchanged during the session, therefore establishing acceptable communication channels. Thus, by playing with her, I learned that the girl had absorbed all the existential malaise of the mother who had never openly spoken about her desperation at having left Italy and all her treasured family connections years earlier, to migrate to a country whose language she had never learned and where she did not want to remain. In other cases, the silence by a family member in session can be a way of "creating an empty space" to contain a very strong emotion, even of joy or gratitude, where words would be out of place. Alternatively, it can be a silence of reconnection or reconciliation between two or more people, who have finally found each other again.

Touching: physical contact in family therapy

Physical contact by the therapist

While touching has been part of most healing traditions throughout human history, it has been controversial in Western medicine and more so, within the field of psychotherapy and counselling. The debate on touching in psychotherapy is generally avoided and the issue of physical contact seems still to be enveloped in a kind of taboo. Even though in the Professional Code of Ethics of the major family associations like the American Family Therapy Academy, the American Association for Marriage and Family Therapy and the European Family Therapy Association there is no specific reference to or prohibition of physical contact in therapy (specific prohibitions refer to sexual activity and everything that, in general, can damage a patient), we are faced with a very sensitive subject. The general opinion in the field of mental health and helping professions is that touching is substantially inappropriate, if we exclude those minimal, ritual ways of greeting clients with a handshake or a pat on the shoulder. For a number of therapists and authors, the fear is that non-sexual touching can easily be transformed to sexual contact with clients (Wolberg, 1967; Pope & Bouhoutsos, 1986; Rutter, 1989; Simon, 1995).

Doubtlessly this implicit prohibition of physical contact in therapy has arisen in recent years because of a series of social and cultural factors. Anglo culture, in particular, had emphasized concepts of autonomy, self-realization and privacy, and most forms of touching in therapy have been perceived as dangerous and potentially sexualized. This is markedly different from Latin and Southern European countries, where touching is much more accepted and welcomed even in a social context as a way of friendly connection. In addition, the skyrocketing of sexual abuse and domestic violence in recent decades has contributed to social alarm and a hyper-protective attitude towards children, both in schools and in public places, and to reinforcement of social stereotypes about men in general, imagined as potential aggressors. As a result, even teachers and psychotherapists are perceived as capable of abusing their authority, and physical contact with children has to be avoided. Furthermore, a heavy burden has been unleashed by a litigious attitude in dealing with controversial treatments. This has resulted in risk management and defensive medical practice, and the consequent conditioning on the part of insurance companies. All this, especially in institutional settings such as hospitals and mental health services, has created heightened fears and defensive attitudes on the part of professionals, who prefer to avoid any physical contact with their clients, because of the potential risk of possible complaints. In addition, touching represents a powerful connection that can produce either positive or negative effects, and many professionals prefer not to take any personal risk and maintain rigid boundaries.

Psychoanalysis never approved of, and eventually entirely prohibited, physical contact in therapy, building up a very rigid setting. At the beginning of his practice, Freud used to touch his patients on the head or the neck, believing that this type of contact would help them to calm down and provide better access to their thoughts (Hunter & Struve, 1998). Later, after incorporating the concept of transference in his theory, he completely changed his attitude, believing that physical contact could interfere with the development of transference (Holub & Lee, 1990). This prohibition conditioned the development of psychoanalysis and of its teaching, and was further reinforced by his student Menninger (1958), who openly condemned any kind of physical contact on the part of the analyst. Things have not changed a great deal in the psychoanalytic field, where non-verbal language and physical contact are still kept out of the therapeutic relationship (Wolberg, 1967; Gutheil & Gabbard, 1993; Bersoff, 1999; Pope & Vasquez, 2007). In different ways, first Ferenczi with his emphasis on self-disclosure and emphatic reciprocity (Rudnytsky, 2000), and later Reich (1972), supporter of touching in psychoanalysis, were for this reason excluded from the Freudian circle.

The development of humanistic theories in the field of Gestalt, transactional analysis and family therapy with an experiential orientation,has contributed to a positive idea about physical contact in therapy. Touching can be a very effective modality in building an intense therapeutic relationship, and in enhancing the therapeutic alliance. It can be very healing for clients who have been suffering very traumatic experiences (Van der Kolk, 2014). Touching is an authentic way of communicating warmth and a sense of trust and safety on the part of the therapist (Satir, 1972; Perls, 1973; Cohen, 1987; Cornell, 1997; Durana, 1998; Smith, Clance & Imes, 1998; Downey, 2001; Field, 2003; Johnson, 2004). Zur (2007), in particular, has been describing touch as a boundary issue, which reflects different cultural traditions as well as distorted cultural and professional views that see boundary crossing as sexual in nature. He makes a clear distinction between "boundary violations", where touching results in totally inappropriate and sexualized behaviour, and "boundary crossing", which, in contrast, enhances an intense affective connection with the client and can include, besides touching, home visits, self-disclosure and the exchange of gifts.

How to make physical contact using your own body

Satir, a Gestalt and family therapist, was an extraordinary model of this way of thinking with her free and intense way of making physical contact with families. Starting from family sculptures, she would physically move and change the position of family members, to provide them with a visual portrait of their underlying dynamics. Haber (2002) described Satir's style very well, and how she modelled appropriate physical contact by using her own body. During a family therapy session, Satir was concerned about the violent behaviour of Jim, an eight-year-old boy, towards his stepmother. She encouraged the boy to touch her own face to teach him how to caress gently, guiding his hands. She then asked Jim to do the same to both his father and stepmother during the same session. The child had been the victim of violent behaviour perpetrated by his biological mother and needed to be re-educated about intimacy, and to experience positive physical contact. The work of Zappella (1987), in holding sessions with autistic children, is very similar to Satir's idea of using her body to model appropriate physical contact. Zappella also taught parents (and even grandparents), who often felt confused and unsure about how to provide physical containment to their autistic children, how to hold them in their arms. He held the child first to demonstrate a safe holding and then asked the parents to do the same.

The "do not be afraid of touching your client" concept has permeated my clinical work with families. Many therapists tend to hide behind a number of justifications for not touching clients, such as: "In the hospital where I work it is forbidden to touch patients"; "According to the law of this state . . . any physical contact with patients is forbidden". Alternatively, they reflect on the potential danger of touching: "What are the consequences of my gesture, if the patient feels humiliated or feels that his personal space has been invaded?" In *The Gift of Therapy*, Yalom (2001) gave a wonderful example of trust and touch in therapy. A middle-aged woman had lost almost all her hair following radiotherapy treatment and always wore a wig. She feared that people (including Yalom) would find her repulsive. Yalom gently encouraged her to remove her wig and reveal her bald head in session. Trusting Yalom gave the woman courage to remove her wig in his presence, allowing him to touch the few remaining hairs on her head. Years later, the woman recounted to him that "touching her hair" had been an action so affirming that it had radically changed the negative image she had of herself.

This example of an intense, profound physical contact reminded me of a case where the wife of a couple I was seeing in therapy came to a session devastated and in total despair. The husband had killed himself by jumping from a bridge. He had casually left the house, saying to his wife that he was going to buy a pack of cigarettes. She stood in front of me, in tears and in deep pain. In respectful silence, I embraced her for a very long time until I felt she was calming down. Then she sat and told me the full story. That embrace, free of therapeutic restraints, gave this woman a sense of relief and much-needed human intimacy, as well as the courage to go on with her life. Years later, she brought to see me her only daughter, who had been a child when the father died. The daughter had asked to meet the person who helped her mother to cope with such a tragedy.

Physical contact: a positive reinforcement of the therapeutic alliance

In our clinical experience, we have considered it very natural to integrate verbal language, the questions we ask members of the family, with body language – eye contact and bodily movements coherent with what we want to convey with our voice and physical contact. This is, without a doubt, a positive reinforcement of the therapeutic relationship, with the power to transmit warmth, presence and sharing, stronger than any words. The examples just given demonstrate the extraordinary effect that touching can produce within an authentic relationship based on mutual trust. Certainly, working with children in therapy has helped me to unblock my "child–creative self" from the excess of "adult–serious self", always present in every therapist's identity, and too often burdened by a sense of duty and responsibility. Even my upbringing in Italy has allowed me to appreciate, since childhood, the language of hands with its innumerable meanings, the potent language of the body and of humour. Sadly, I have to admit that this kind of cultural heritage made up of daily life experiences, rich and varied in every culture, is often not utilized in therapy. It is almost as if many therapists have been discouraged from incorporating their authentic selves, giving up jokes, humour and everyday spontaneous behaviour, in order to build a detached "therapeutic person". There are many symbolic ways of greeting, such as shaking hands, high-fiving young people or a pat on the shoulder that may be viewed simply as common ritualistic ways of taking leave. In fact, even these greetings can convey very meaningful messages. For example, the warmth and strength of a father's handshake at the end of a session can communicate a feeling of gratitude towards the therapist, satisfaction about what happened in the meeting or a gesture to confirm a desire to engage in therapy. The same applies to "giving a high-five" to an adolescent, or a pat on the shoulder, as if to say: "We did it!"

I have been using physical contact in therapy in many different ways, according to the affective context of the session and the goals for therapy. I might ask a child or adolescent to move from his chair and come closer to me. This movement can be followed by a complicit glance and a physical contact to transmit an affective connection or the understanding of a relational difficulty. At other times, touching can represent a kind of challenge to confront a child with a specific issue: a plastic hammer, an axe or a sword can be used to connect physically and mimic fighting.

In a therapeutic situation, described earlier in this book, an adolescent called his father by phone, asking him to attend therapy. Once the father arrived at the session, I gently took the boy's hand to show the father's mobile number written on his son's palm. This contact of support was a way to amplify the importance of the father's presence in the session in that moment, and to transmit to the son a message of validation of his courageous and heartfelt initiative.

I remember in another consultation in Chile, South America, working with an adolescent boy who had become involved in street gangs. During the course of one of these street fights, he had been stabbed in the chest, and nearly died. He attended the session with his parents. They were extremely concerned about their son and had grave fears for his future. I remember gently touching the extensive scar on his chest, and asking him what would have happened to his parents if the knife had struck his heart, and he had died. This intimate physical contact allowed me to tackle the family's dilemma in a very direct way. It also conveyed an implicit message to the adolescent boy, that he needed to take better care of himself, or the next time he might not be so lucky.

In a consultation with a coloured family from South Africa, I was working with a very angry 14-year-old adolescent girl and her two much younger sisters, whom she claimed she despised. I asked her if she thought her sisters liked her. She said, "probably not". I said, "Maybe they are scared of you and your angry mask?" I asked her to allow her two young sisters to sit on her lap and to stroke their heads gently. She demonstrated trust in me by her willingness to do as I had asked, but pushed her body away from her sisters and placed her hands claw-like on their heads. I got up, moved behind her and crouched down on the floor beside her, and coached her in how to touch her sisters' heads gently, by unclawing her fingers and directing her hands to stroke her sisters' heads. The adolescent girl had tears in her eyes when she did this. Her sisters sat quite woodenly on her lap but they did not move away. I gave words to what was unspoken in her heart: "You need this, you miss this, they need this, they miss this". I also asked the girl's mother to cradle her on her lap and to touch her with love.

In other sessions, I touched the scars on the arms of a desperate, self-harming girl to convey my emotional connection with her. I touched the tattoos on the arms of a young man and expressed curiosity about their symbolic meaning to him, and asked about the colour of nail polish on the nails of a little girl who played at being grown up, while gently holding her hand. In all these cases, the appropriate and gentle use of physical touch communicated my desire to enter deeply into my client's experience of life.

Contact can be mediated through the exchange of objects – parts of clothing such as a hat, a scarf or a shoe, that can be taken and passed to another family member – to facilitate a process of identification and connection between family members. We have also discussed how to form an alliance by "doing together". It can be seen, thus, that the desire to transmit a message of understanding through physical contact can be transmitted by the way in which we construct a geno-gram, handle family photographs, formulate a contract or finish with a handshake. Touching is always a gentle, yet powerful, way to connect with a family member in particular, but it also conveys a message of empathy and support for the whole family.

Taking the locket in my hands and speaking to the mother

Liliana, a woman with strongly hysterical traits, was referred to therapy because she was "ruining her family". She was convinced that the husband's family had "put a curse" on her and that the house was "haunted by demons". The husband, who had built the family house with his hands, and their two adolescent sons were mute and very impotent in the face of Liliana's allegations. Instead of entering into her crazy thoughts, I expressed curiosity about a pendant she was wearing. This request changed the entire climate of the session. The pendant was a locket with a small picture of her mother, who had died recently. I got closer to her and asked to see it. She took it off carefully and very delicately placed it in my hands. Realizing that Liliana had never recovered from that loss, I began to "speak with the mother", who had left behind a terrible void. From the moment that I "took her mother into my hands" and started to speak to her as if she were still alive, a process of affiliation began with Liliana, who trusted me completely. That allowed me to move, step by step, to restore harmony in the family, and to re-establish fam-ily boundaries and priorities. Therapy lasted for more than a year, but our physical contact through the locket was a key turning point, a sign of mutual understanding that remained active even after therapy was concluded. In fact, Liliana kept sending postcards and letters of gratitude to me for a few years after.

Physical contact to rebuild connections

Physical contact is one of the essential elements in human development, a pro-found way of communicating, a fundamental component in the health and devel-opment of the child and a powerful force in healing illness (Bowlby & Robertson, 1952). Montagu (1971) described touch as the first language and the mother of all senses because it is the first sense to develop in the embryo. He outlined that a lack of tactile stimuli in infancy gave rise to an inability to establish relationships involv-ing touch with others. Starting from these premises, studies on baby observation in attachment theory have led to extraordinary results in the understanding of child development.

I have always believed that physical connection has a fundamental place and value in healing old but still open wounds, and in rebuilding trust in much-damaged relationships. This belief has definitely been confirmed in my clinical experience of working with families from around the world. My model teaches therapists to find the motivation and the courage to demolish defensive barriers and prejudices crystallized over time, and to build new relational bridges in order to reconstruct family bonds. Many fears, hidden desires, emotional disconnections, myths and family secrets reappear during the course of therapy, and this *unfinished business* of the past can find, through present difficulties, an opportunity for resolution. The reconstruction of interrupted bonds mainly pertains to the world of adults, but has significant repercussions in couples' relationships, in parenting and in the general wellbeing and health of children. For anyone who has not had her primary needs for care and love met during her upbringing, therapy with the family can be a safe and welcoming context for repairing interrupted or damaged bonds. This healing through touching in therapy represents the best treatment for resolving inter-generational conflicts and couples' crises. Let us look at an example.

Meeting the mother after 30 years

Leonardo came to family therapy with his wife Lara and their 20-year-old only son, Giovanni. The presenting issue was Giovanni's aggressive behaviour. Giovanni used drugs and did not accept any rules at home, provoking and threatening his father in every way, with the implicit support of his mother, who protected him from his father's fury. Even in session, father and son replayed their verbal abuse of each other, with Lara, the mother, always taking her son's side, even though she was in denial about doing so. Leonardo was anxious and easily angered; the marriage had been in crisis for a long time, and Giovanni behaved as though he wanted the family to explode. In exploring the father's history, I learnt that Leonardo left his family at the age of 15 to enrol in the army because of constant fights in his family of origin, but above all because he felt his mother never loved him or took care of him. In therapy, Leonardo outlined his experiences of neglect. He said that he remembered that, as a baby, his mother had kept him in a horrible cot and never even changed his nappies. He was extremely resentful of his mother and, in fact, had not seen her for over 30 years, even though they lived in the same city. His siblings, in contrast, had continued to have frequent contact with her. Leonardo's parents separated when he was an adolescent, but had since reunited.

After working with this family for approximately a year and having earned the father's full trust, I encouraged Leonardo to arrange a special encounter with his mother. Actually, for that special meeting, I asked him to bring in his whole family of origin, including his father and siblings. I was pleasantly surprised by his acceptance of my invitation, which taught me never to underestimate what we can ask of families in order to rebuild affective ties. Leonardo warned me that his mother Giulia, now elderly, had been a theatre actress, and that she was still playing the "prima donna" in the family. Giulia came to the session carrying a large bag full of letters, documents and cards she had collected to demonstrate what a loving mother she had been to her son, the eldest of five. Naturally, Leonardo contested every point, and their old war was replayed in session, resulting in further disconnection and new resentments. It was difficult to imagine they had not seen each other for 30 years! Time had stood still for mother and son since he left home at the age of 15, and the ensuing 30 years had been filled with ongoing assumptions, resentments and affective distance on both sides. My goal for this session was to change the affective context from one of a judicious courtroom battle to an opportunity for healing and repair of a bond that had remained broken for so many years. My belief that this was possible was upheld by the fundamental fact that the son had invited the mother and that she had accepted his invitation.

Mother and son were sitting at opposite ends of the family group. I decided to use myself as a bridge. I moved the son between the mother and myself. This movement alone produced a positive emotion in both of them, as it represented the possibility of a connection they both feared and desired. I then took Leonardo's hand and placed it in his mother's hand, holding both within my own hands, in an affectionate, yet firm, hold. As neither of them pulled away, I took it as a positive sign to continue holding them together. The mother felt the need to speak and revisit the key aspects of the family drama. She spoke painfully of her memory of her husband hitting her when Leonardo was 14 years old and that, instead of defending her, Leonardo told the father to "let her have more!" At this recollection of a painful event in the family's life, Leonardo turned his head away and let go of his mother's hand. I reminded the mother that this was a special occasion, not only to recount the abuse she had suffered, but also to listen to her son's voice after 30 years. The mother was able to collect herself and looked into her son's eyes with a loving smile. She took his hand in hers and, for the first time, was silent. Leonardo responded positively to her caring look, smiled back, and concluded this moment of newfound intimacy with a hug. Leonardo was then able to say:

> I realize that as a son perhaps I could have or should have defended you on that and other occasions. I did not do so and I am very sorry about it; I ask your forgiveness. I am here now to tell you that I do not hate you and no longer resent you: we have found each other again and we hugged. That is all good! However, this does not mean that we can re-establish a normal relationship, because that would be hypocritical of me. The best I can do is tell you from the heart that I don't hate you, I never hated you and that I wish you only the best.

The mother then embraced him and they exchanged an affectionate kiss on the cheek. At the end of the meeting, Leonardo held her coat while she dressed and held her hand while he accompanied her out of the therapy room. Lara also took part in the session, and for the first time, she heard and understood what her husband had carried around inside him for years. This session had a profound impact on the following session, attended by Lara, Leonardo and their son. Giovanni had not been present at the meeting with his father's family of origin, but was able to imagine what Leonardo had felt in that meeting with his mother. This had the effect of helping Giovanni really to appreciate his father, who had taken such a big personal risk and demonstrated incredible courage. Leonardo looked like someone who had just scaled a high mountain, exhausted but happy to have reached his goal, and Lara, for the first time, saw her husband in a new light.

A warm embrace between brother and sister

Helping two people, who have built over the years an affective barrier between them, to reconnect in front of other family members is a very effective way of repairing broken affective bonds. This can be said of Edith and Patrick, two siblings who competed for their mother's affection through their respective illnesses (this case has already been discussed in Chapter 7). Patrick suffered from a congenital pancreatic disease, while Edith had more recently developed severe anorexia. At the end of the session, I asked them to show concretely what their affective distance was now, using the space between their two chairs as a measure of the distance. They moved their chairs closer to each other, maintaining a relatively safe distance. I then asked them what closeness they wished to achieve in order to feel comfortable with each other and, at this point, they moved so close that they were physically in contact. Encouraged by their mutual desire to feel close, I asked them to demonstrate their affection for each other physically and they put their arms around each other's shoulders, with immense pleasure. They continued the session holding hands, and this experience of a strong emotional connection marked the beginning of a transformation in the sibling relationship and that of the whole family.

This idea of facilitating not only a symbolic or verbal reconnection between estranged family members, but also encouraging a concrete expression of it in session has become a constant theme in my therapeutic work. I am convinced that therapy, being itself a kind of ritual, allows for various expressions of intimate contact to take place during a session. These expressions form part of a therapeutic ritual that becomes engraved in the memory of the person experiencing this first hand, and of the entire family, who are privileged witnesses to a collective transformation. Sealing a newfound affective bond with an affectionate gesture, a warm and prolonged embrace, or by laughing or crying together permits incredible transformations to take place in the individual, and the therapist can then use himself as a bridge to reconnect disconnected parts of the family system.

Case example: Rob's burdens

This chapter will end with segments from a family consultation, which illustrates the philosophy of my method of intervention and outlines some of the main ideas presented in this book:

1. the construction of a therapeutic alliance with a seven-year-old child, Rob, through words, non-verbal language and physical contact;
2. playing with the concrete metaphor of the weight that Rob symbolically carries on his shoulders as a challenge to his parenting functions;

3. the search for adult resources among his mother's sisters to support her emotionally;
4. the description of the mother's story of resilience and of the unprocessed grief regarding her husband's tragic death at the birth of the second child, Tommy;
5. the significance of Rob's smile, reflected in the father's smiling photograph.

The family's history

Rob's father, following a terrible car accident, went into a coma and died a few months later, immediately after Tommy's birth. Rob was two years old at the time of his father's death. The mother was left alone to bring up the two boys and initiated family therapy because of Rob's poor academic performance and his withdrawal at school. The therapist, who requested a consultation with me, had been helping the family for two years, alternating joint sessions with individual ones with Rob or his mother. At the start of the consultation I (identified as C in the dialogue) asked the mother how I might help the therapist with Rob's problems. The mother responded with a positive description of the child.

Who can help Mum besides Rob?

Mother:	"Rob is a very sensitive child!"
C (inviting the slender, lanky child who is playing in the room):	"Come here; let me have a look at you! (taking the child's wrist as if checking his pulse) It is true! You are a very sensitive child (speaking gently and looking him in the eyes), but you are also a very good child with fantastic blue eyes. I think you are taking very good care of your mother. Is that true? Is it your job to take care of your mother? Did you know you are the big boy in the family? You have a big responsibility on your shoulders! Do you have strong shoulders? Can we see if your shoulders are that strong?"
	(The child appeared to be almost hypnotized. This strange "doctor" seemed to be able to look into his soul and to name the role he has assumed in the family, that of protecting his mother. He does not pull back from the playful physical contact with the doctor. Nor later, when "the doctor" gently pressed down on his shoulders to check how robust they are.)
C:	"Gosh, they are really strong! Like a rock! Who else can help your mum besides you? Are you alone? Or, do you want to be alone?" (Rob nods)
C:	It is a lot of work, Hmm. How old are you?"
Rob:	"Seven."
C:	"For a seven-year-old it is a lot of work . . . Have you ever asked your mum's sisters to help you?"
Rob:	"No."

C:	"Never? Who else can help Mum? I have an idea. (There is a small child-sized table with chairs in the room, with paper and coloured pencils.) Please sit on that chair; you have to help me . . . You have to write on the paper . . . What colour do you prefer?"
Rob:	"Green."
C (indicating the paper):	"We need to write here: Help for mummy, in your language."
	(Rob begins to write in a beautiful hand).
C:	"You write very well, you are a good student! Now, under the title you should make a list of the people who can help Mummy. You are the first. Who comes after you?"
	(In the meantime Tommy, curious about his brother's home-work, approaches the table and is invited to sit down and col-laborate, also by writing something.)
C:	"I think I can understand your language, let me see . . . Rob is you, Tommy is he, and this is Mum's sister Rachel? Therefore, we already have three people who are helping Mummy; can we also include her (indicating the therapist)? She helps Mummy, is she good?"
	(Rob nods his head.)
C	(looking at the names the child has written down): "Is this a dif-ferent auntie or is she the same one?
Mother:	"I have four sisters, but they are all busy with their families!"
C:	"After this meeting, do you think that Sue [the therapist] can ask Rachel to come and help you and Mummy?
Rob:	"I don't know, yet."
C:	"I think you do not trust your auntie too much; you want to do everything yourself. True? Mummy is yours, hmm. The only one who can help you a bit is your little brother!"

Is it possible to smile with 50 kilos on your shoulders?

C (addressing the mother):	"So, these wonderful children have grown up so well because of you? You did a good job! Are you satisfied . . . are you proud of yourself?"
Mother:	"Yes."
	(Up to this point Rob has maintained a serious expression, show-ing no hint of a smile and the mother confirms that Rob laughs very seldom, even at home.)
C:	"But can you smile with 50 kilos on your shoulders? If Rob thinks he can take these 50 kilos off his shoulders he might be able to smile. We need to do some magic (holding a magic wand in his hand, he points to the child's back). Now these 50 kilos must disap-pear! Here is the deal! You have 50 kilos on your shoulders, whom can we give them back to? Wait, I want to show you something."

	(The consultant gets up and goes to the other side of the room where there is a rucksack full of recording equipment belonging to the video operator, who is taping the session; he picks it up and asks Rob to lift it.)
C:	"This rucksack is very heavy! Try to lift it."
	(Rob lifts it as if it does not weigh too much.)
C:	"Heavy?"
Rob:	"A bit."
C:	"Only a bit? Mum, could you check the weight? He says only a bit."
Mother:	"It is heavy!"
C (addressing the therapist):	"You check it too, Sue."
Sue:	"It is very heavy!"
C:	"And he said only a bit! It is very heavy and you will become a weight-lifting champion. How can you smile with all this weight on your shoulders? Let us see if we can do some magic."
Rob (boasting):	"I can lift even two rucksacks!"
C:	"You can lift two rucksacks? Like this one? You really are a strong boy! Well, Mum, can we do this magic? Usually when a young boy loses his father, he needs his mother and the other adults in the family to help him grow. It is the same for Tommy, but he knows he cannot carry such a big weight. That is why he can smile."
	(As if to confirm this, Tommy flashes him a beautiful smile.)
C:	"Are you a bit worried about him, Mum?"
Mother:	"Yes, I'm very worried about Rob."
C:	"But are you more worried about him or yourself?"
Mother:	"About him."
C (pointing at Tommy):	"And, about him?"
Mother:	"Less so."
C:	"So, you are worried about him and he worries about you! How can we solve this problem? He has been worried about you since the day he was born. You are worried about him from the moment he was born. Well, two worries are not helpful. We have to widen the frame of who can help this family. You two are too alike. Very sensitive, very sad and very connected. Did you know this? Did you know that you and Mum are very similar?"

The mother's burdens

C:	"So you too, Jenny [mother], carry a big weight?"
Jenny:	"Very big."
C:	"When you were a little girl, at Rob's age, how much weight did you carry?"

Jenny:	"A lot."
C (pointing at Rob):	"Does he know that?"
Jenny:	"No."
C:	"Do you think you can tell him, now?"
Jenny:	"I told him that I did not have a good mother."
C:	"What does 'not a good mother' mean?"
Jenny:	"She always left me alone, she abandoned me and I had to manage alone."
C:	"So your mother did not die but she was not available."
Jenny:	"Yes."
C:	"Was it always so?"
Jenny:	"Yes, since I was very small."
C (addressing Rob):	"Did you know this?"
Rob:	"No."
Jenny (embracing Tommy, who is cuddling up to her):	"I didn't even have a good father, he was an alcoholic and, being the eldest, I took care of everyone, five sisters and one brother."
C:	"So who can help you now?"
Jenny:	"That is a big question!"
C:	"Do you allow people like your sisters to help?"
Jenny:	"I live half an hour from my sisters, but during the week we do not get to see each; they all work and have children."
C:	"This sounds like an excuse. If they needed your help, would you give it?"
Jenny:	"I would run to their aid!"
C:	"So you are better at giving than receiving!"
Jenny:	"I always worry that I do not give the utmost to my children."
C:	"You are so loyal to your children; you certainly did not have good parents, but you want to be a perfect parent to them, to give them the best. Have you ever thought that if you were happier and less sad, they would benefit?"

It is hard after six years of isolation

Jenny:	"Yes, I think about it, but it is hard after six years of isolation."
C:	"You are still very sad at losing your husband?"
Jenny:	"Yes."
C:	"Was he a good husband?"
Jenny:	"Yes."
C:	"And a good father, too? Even though it was for only a short time?"

Jenny:	"Yes."
C:	"Do you have a photo of him with you? Do the children look like him?"
Jenny:	"Rob looks very much like him; Tommy looks like my husband's mother. Rob has his father's eyes and hair."
C (addressing Rob and holding the father's photo next to his face):	"Come here. Look at your dad and now try to smile like him; let me see your smile. (For the first time Rob, visibly moved, gives him a beautiful smile.) How beautiful! You really look like him! Mummy does not know that the happier she is, the happier you will be!"

Suggestion for the therapist

C (addressing Sue):	"I would concentrate less on the school problems, forget the school, he is a good student! He has to unload all that weight, and then he will be a good child in everything he does. Now he is a little sad and has good reason to be. This family needs an injection of hope, light-heartedness, vitality and play. We need to 'open the house' and reactivate the relationship with the sisters and help Jenny to ask for help for herself, to find time to process her grief after such an important loss. Only then will she be able to smile at life again. And Rob will give himself permission to smile too."

Follow-up session

Sue met with the family two months later, and reported that everyone spoke enthusiastically about the session, and that Rob's face lit up every time they spoke about the consultation. From the session, the mother had a clearer understanding of the impact of her husband's death on the children and herself, the lack of support in her life and how her son was trying to compensate for her emotional loss. In terms of future therapy, plans included for the mother to have individual sessions with Sue to help her work through her grief, and to invite her sisters and a couple of friends to the sessions to find new resources for the family. Following my suggestion, Sue also had plans to ask a male co-therapist to assist in family therapy sessions, in order to provide a male presence to support her sons better.

References

Bersoff, D. N. (Ed.) (1999). *Ethical Conflicts in Psychology*. Washington, DC: American Psychological Association.

Bowen, M. (1978). *Family Therapy in Clinical Practice*. New York: Jason Aronson.

Bowlby, J. & Robertson, J. (1952). A Two-year-old Goes to Hospital. *Proceedings of the Royal Society of Medicine, 46*, 425–427.

Cohen, S. S. (1987). *The Magic of Touch*. New York: Harper and Row.

Cornell, W. F. (1997). Touch and Boundaries in Transactional Analysis: Ethical and Transferential Considerations. *Transactional Analysis Journal, 37*(1), 30–37.

Di Nicola, V. F. (1985). The Acoustic Mask: A Review of Behind the Family Mask. *Journal of Strategic & Systemic Therapies*, 4(1), 74–80.

Downey, D. L. (2001). Therapeutic Touch in Psychotherapy. *Psychotherapy*, 36(1), 35–38.

Durana, C. (1998). The Use of Touch in Psychotherapy: Ethical and Clinical Guidelines. *Psychotherapy*, 35(1), 269–280.

Field, T. (2003). *Touch*. Cambridge, MA: MIT Press.

Gutheil, T. G. & Gabbard, G. O. (1993). The Concept of Boundaries in Clinical Practice: Theoretical and Risk-Management Dimensions. *American Journal of Psychiatry*, 150, 188–196.

Haber, R. (2002). Virginia Satir: An Integrated, Humanistic Approach. *Contemporary Family Therapy*, 24(1), 23–34.

Holub, E. A., & Lee, S. S. (1990). Therapist's Use of Non-erotic Physical Contact: Ethical Concerns. *Professional Psychology: Research and Practice*, 21, 115–117.

Hunter, M. & Struve, J. (1998). *The Ethical Use of Touch in Psychotherapy*. Thousand Oaks, CA: Sage Publications.

Johnson, S. M. (2004). *Creating Connection: The Practice of Emotionally Focused Marital Therapy*. New York: Brunner/Routledge.

Menninger, K. (1958). *Theory of Psychoanalytic Technique*. New York: Science Edition.

Montagu, A. (1971).*Touching: The Human Significance of the Skin*. New York: Harper & Row.

Perls, F. (1973). *The Gestalt Approach and Eye Witness to Therapy*. Palo Alto, CA: Science & Behavior Books.

Pope, K. S. & Bouhoutsos, J. (1986). *Sexual Intimacy Between Therapists and Patients*. New York: Praeger.

Pope, K. S. & Vasquez, M. J. T. (2007). *Ethics in Therapy and Counselling: A Practical Guide* (3rd ed.). San Francisco: Jossey-Bass.

Reich, W. (1972). *Character Analysis*. New York: Simon & Schuster.

Rogers, C. R. (1951). *Client-centered Psychotherapy*. Boston: Houghton Mifflin.

Roustang, F. (2014). *Feuilles Oubliées, Feuilles Retrouvées*. Paris : Payot & Rivages.

Rudnytsky, P. L. (2000). *Ferenczi's Turn in Psychoanalysis*. New York: University Press.

Rutter, P. (1989). *Sex in the Forbidden Zone*. London: Harper Collins.

Satir, V. (1972). *Peoplemaking*. Palo Alto, CA: Science and Behavior Books.

Simon, R. I. (1995). The Natural History of Therapist Sexual Misconduct. Identification and Prevention. *Psychiatric Annals*, 25, 90–94.

Smith, E., Clance, P. R. & Imes, S. (Eds.) (1998). *Touch in Psychotherapy: Theory, Research and Practice*. New York: Guilford Press.

Stern, D. (2010). *Forms of Vitality: Exploring Dynamic Experience in Psychology, the Arts, Psychotherapy, and Development*. New York: Oxford University Press.

Van Der Kolk, B. (2014). *The Body Keeps the Score*. New York: Penguin.

Watzlawick, P., Beavin, J. H. & Jackson, D. D. (1967). *Pragmatic of Human Communication. A Study of Interactional Patterns, Pathologies, and Paradoxes*. New York: Norton.

Wolberg, L. (1967). *The Technique of Psychotherapy* (2nd Ed.). New York: Grune & Stratton.

Yalom, I. D. (2001). *The Gift of Therapy*. New York: Harper Collins Publishers.

Zappella, M. (1987). *I Bambini Autistici, l'Holding e la Famiglia*. Rome: Nuova Italia Scientifica.

Zur, O. (2007). *Boundaries in Psychotherapy: Ethical and Clinical Explorations*. Washington, DC: APA Books.

10

THE HUMAN DIMENSION IN PSYCHOTHERAPY AND RESEARCH

During the 1970s, an entire generation of psychiatrists and psychologists in the Western world rebelled against the internment of patients into lunatic asylums and other forms of physical and pharmacological restraint. Social community psychiatry and family therapy were born and developed from the failure of a model of intervention based on social exclusion and marginalization of mentally ill patients. It has taken a long time to heal the relationship between normality and pathology, and to allow the human resources inside the illness to emerge. It has taken just as long to discover and concretely demonstrate that the cure is not only to be found inside the patient, but also within the family, in the social context and in human solidarity.

In our clinical work, we have experienced that the voices of children and adolescents *must* be listened to within the context of the family, the school and therapeutic institutions. Psychological and psychosomatic disturbances in children are often strong indicators of familial distress that go beyond their present difficulties. Listening to their voices in family therapy often allows important transformations to occur on many levels. It also paves the way for the rapid resolution of adolescents' or children's symptoms by intervening on more relevant and often dramatic realities (Andolfi & Mascellani, 2013).

The limit of the medical model in treating mental and relational problems

In the last few decades, the medical model has been expanding beyond the boundaries of pure medical conditions, influencing psychiatry heavily towards a biological orientation. These days, even healthy people are conditioned to search for magic solutions to prevent or eliminate sadness, unhappiness, and loss of sexual desire, grief, old age, anxiety and loneliness. "Scientifically tested" medications and manuals such as the fifth edtion of the *Diagnostic and Statistical Manual of Mental Disorders* (DSM-5: American Psychiatric Association, 2013) attempt to extend the medical-psychiatric model to include virtually all human behaviours into a classificatory bible. Diagnosis and the use of medications are out of control. The boundaries of psychiatry have been stretched, and normality is becoming ever more restricted. According to Frances (2013), an eminent psychiatrist and one of the editors responsible for the fourth edition of the DSM (American Psychiatric Association, 1994), 20 per cent of the adult population is said to suffer from some kind of mental disorder, and another 20 per cent takes psycho-pharmaceuticals. Furthermore, nowadays there are *smart pills*, designed to provide cognitive improvement to promote optimal functioning for people such as surgeons, pilots or entrepreneurs, not to mentions masses of students who fill themselves with amphetamines to face stressful exams. Beyond the supposed efficacy of these drugs, what is truly concerning is the life philosophy that pushes people to be "superheroes". The message in society is for the need to succeed at all costs, without weakness or failure. However, what are the ethical implications of these "scientific discoveries"?

Family therapy was born in the United States in the middle of the 1960s and spread throughout the Western world. However, now that it is strongly in decline in its birthplace, it is beginning to assume new and vital dimensions in Asian countries, where the family therapy movement seems to have taken root and become more relevant. We cannot forget that one of the reasons why family therapy has lost its impetus in the United States was due to the tenacious opposition demonstrated by the Association of the Families of the Mentally Ill towards therapists, who were accused, not unjustly, of having blamed parents for their children's mental dysfunctions.

The advent of neuroscience and studies in brain functioning have opened an area of incredible research (think about the discovery of mirror neurons), and clinical experimentation with the possibility of finding effective cures for illnesses like Parkinson's disease, Alzheimer's disease and autism. Concurrently, these neurobiological studies have provided backing for the exponential growth and indiscriminate use of psycho-pharmaceuticals in the treatment of many forms of psychopathology, to the point of prescribing antidepressants in massive dosages to children affected by attention-deficit hyperactivity disorder and other dysfunctions. Social psychiatry and even psychodynamic modalities have lost power, and the new generation of psychiatrists seems to believe almost exclusively in the more drastic solutions provided by biological treatment. Individual assessments and pathological labelling of people, together with the abuse of pharmaceuticals, have conditioned the orientation of treating institutions and professionals, and shackled their capacity to look beyond the symptoms of the single individual, fragmenting families, without looking at their human, affective and competent dimensions. In this panorama, research on the effectiveness of family psychotherapy is very much needed to show evidence of an alternative way of curing clients, using the family as the main resource for recovery, more than just labelling and medicating symptoms.

Research on the effectiveness of family therapy

Certainly, psychotherapy suffers from a notable historical delay in putting in place shared and demonstrable evaluation criteria on the efficacy of therapy. Only in recent years has family therapy produced significant research on the evaluation of results, recognized by the scientific community and the sector's associations. Still, few research projects include an active participation of families after treatment, in the construction of criteria, in order to evaluate therapeutic results, with the implicit assumption that only professionals know how to select and organize research data with scientific evidence.

The resistance to evaluate psychotherapeutic results

The answer to this delay can be attributed to various factors. Psychoanalysis, the original source from which psychotherapy stemmed, had for many decades avoided any codified form of evaluation of the results of individual therapy. The concept of confidentiality and the lack of external reporting about the progress of therapy prevented parents, spouses or colleagues from receiving information regarding the individual's change in therapy, as though they were undesirable intrusions. The concept of confidentiality still underpins the vast majority of individual therapy, as though there is a secretiveness about establishing a rapport with the deepest and most private aspects of the individual, that is totally separate from the wider community the individual belongs to. Even if the client reports about the results achieved through therapy, it would still fall short of "social proof", the confirmation of individual change by family members and wider social network. In addition, the description of therapeutic outcomes is strongly influenced by the therapist's own subjectivity.

A second reason for the complexity in evaluating the efficacy of family psychotherapy is the fact that we often use the same criteria employed in individual therapy to measure therapeutic alliance, resolution of symptoms and change. An individual can describe with relative ease the quality of the therapeutic relationship, his process of joining and quality of alliance with the therapist, the resolution of symptoms and the results achieved. It is quite different to adopt evaluation criteria that allow for formalized reports about therapeutic success formulated by two partners (couple therapy), or by different members (family therapy). If family therapy has as its objective individual behaviour modification or symptoms resolution, it is not hard to ask the client whether treatment has been satisfactory and it would be simple to ask for the family's opinion once the symptoms have disappeared. This is the reason why it is not difficult to evaluate brief focused, strategic and cognitive therapies. However, the criteria to describe the therapy's effectiveness would be very different when we expect a transformative process of the whole family and not just the remission of individual symptoms. In this case, when faced with a request for intervention in a couple in crisis or for serious disorders in a child or adolescent, the individual symptoms will only be the "tip of the iceberg", because, once observed and understood, we will then need to deal with the iceberg in its totality.

Pioneering research in the field of family therapy

Pinsof has been a pioneer in the field of research about family therapy process and outcomes at the Family Institute of Northwestern University. In collaboration with

Greenberg, he edited a well-known research handbook on *The Psychotherapeutic Process* (Pinsof & Greenberg, 1986). Later on, he looked for an integration with biological psychotherapy (Pinsof, 1995), and then tried to bridge the gap between clinical practice and research in collaboration with Wynne (Pinsof & Wynne, 2000), and, more recently, described the *Integrative Problem Centered Meta-frameworks Therapy* (Breunlin, Pinsof & Russell, 2011). In recent years, the attention of researchers has focused more on the study of the quality of the therapeutic relationship and on the elements that constitute the alliance between the therapist and the family. Friedlander, Escudero and Heatherington (2005) have developed a model called *SOFTA* (System for Observing Family Therapy Alliance), designed to study the quality of interactions between the various members of the family, as well as of that between each family member and the therapist. Duncan, Miller and Sparks (2000) pursued the same objective in *The Heroic Client*. They described a revolutionary way of improving the effectiveness of interventions through therapy centred on the client, and on the evaluation of results by each member of the family at the end of each session. Thus, through feedback from the family, the therapist was able to evaluate how to proceed or change her lines of intervention, favouring greater involvement and direction by the family in session, in order to reach the proposed objectives.

The study of therapeutic alliance is also at the basis of research on the primary triangle by Fivaz-Depeursinge and Corboz-Warnery (1999), that focused on the micro-analytic observation of triadic interactions between infant, mother and father. This clinical research model was later extended to include pre-school children in so-called Lausanne Triangle Play, described by Fivaz-Depeursinge and Philipp in *The Baby and the Couple* (2014). Carr (2009a, b) has been conducting a large investigation into the effectiveness of family therapy for child-focused problems as well as for adults, published in the same issue of the *Journal of Family Therapy*. In both articles, he presents evidence from meta-analysed, systematic literature reviews and controlled trials for the effectiveness of couple and family therapy for adults and children with various relational and mental health problems. More recently, Sexton and Datchi (2014) wrote about the development and evolution of family therapy research and its impact on practice and future direction in the field of family therapy. An attempt to integrate practice and clinical research is described in the section below, where families, after treatment, took a central role in correcting and expanding our research criteria and reflecting on the efficacy of our practice.

An attempt to include families in long-term follow-up clinical research

In *The Myth of Atlas* (Andolfi, Angelo & de Nichilo, 1989), we discussed the criteria that underpinned follow-up sessions of family therapy treatments. Our goal was to check individual changes, including the disappearance of the symptoms for which therapy was sought, as well as a transformation in the family's relational patterns. After the publication of that volume, we worked for a further 12 years with a qualitative research project on the follow-up of family treatments (Andolfi, Angelo & D'Atena, 2001), counting on a sample of 150 couples and families to be interviewed at a distance of three to four years from the end of therapy. Unfortunately, this book has never been translated into English. We engaged a group of researchers/psychologists who investigated and conducted interviews by phone, by video-recorded follow-up sessions, with both families and therapists, separately, in order to collate the reflections of the entire therapeutic system. The objective of this research was first to explore the outcome of the presenting individual issue for which the family went to therapy. Then, we wanted to know how the family had changed over the years, what memories each of them had about the therapy, which sessions or specific situations were perceived as more transformative or difficult to handle. The same types of questions were also asked of the therapist to explore his memory about individual and family satisfaction about the therapeutic process. We wanted to know also when he felt any sort of blockage or impasse during the course of therapy. In the case of couple therapy the interview procedure was much the same. Phone interviews were conducted separately with each of the partners, while face-to-face contact happened with both partners present.

We cannot report the results of a monumental project in a few lines, but I would like to relate some of the general impressions. First, we discovered the social value of conducting this research project. The families we interviewed came to therapy because of a long and painful history of mental disorders, psychosomatic or relational disturbances in one or more of their members. A few years later, after the conclusion of therapy, they accepted with a sense of gratitude and great pleasure our invitation to a follow-up session, stating that their reflection on the experience of therapy and their description of the results achieved would be useful to other families in distress. Furthermore, the memory of the most significant therapeutic passages helped us therapists to understand better the usefulness and timing of our interventions. For example, several clients reported that the most important and challenging sessions were those where the family of origin was invited to attend. This confirmed our assumptions about the transformative power of these encounters. It also provided feedback on the importance of preparing well for these meetings and the right timing of the invitation. Otherwise, the risk of a therapeutic impasse could be very high. We received relevant validation on the usefulness of non-verbal language and of family sculptures as emotional maps of the relationships in the family. Very powerful images from the sculptures, together with the evocative power of metaphorical objects used in therapy, remained imprinted in the collective memories of the family for a long time. Those objects, once introduced in the session, assumed the most diverse relational meanings. Families reported how significantly fears, hopes and desires for change had become embodied in them.

We understood once more that a solid therapeutic alliance and a climate of safety and trust in the session were essential to confront painful and at times dramatic issues and were the central pivot of change. Several families reported that the therapist's presence and personal commitment to the family were of fundamental importance for the journey of healing. They also reported that essential questions, interventions or specific suggestions were perceived as reassuring or, other times, very challenging, and helped them to get unstuck. We received confirmation in our belief that considerable time is needed to consolidate the progress initiated in therapy. We noted that, in those situations where therapy had been satisfactory, the memories of the family members were very similar to those of the therapist, as though a strong affective resonance had been created within the therapeutic system. Lastly, the families who were able to join forces together and use their resources in therapy most successfully were the ones who achieved the best results. In the follow-up sessions, they were happy to show these positive changes, visible through their body language, their posture and their looks. Couples also described the lengthy and complex paths of their changes both individually and of finding each other again as a couple, happy to have made it after the lessons learnt in therapy. Even those couples that chose separation were happy to have closed a chapter of their lives without resentment and without involving their children in the process of affective separation.

The recovery of Thomas: a miracle or a healing therapeutic process?

I like to close this volume with the description of a very special therapeutic experience with a young adult, Thomas, and his desperate parents. There is a current pattern to disregard adverse family life experiences as problems to be investigated in therapy, and to limit the assessment to the specific disorders that need treatment. The case of Thomas provides a good example of another way to "base our evidence" of therapeutic efficacy and result, so different from the dominant medical model. In fact, the story of Thomas and his family offers a direct challenge to the arrogance and limitation of our psychiatric tools in assessing and treating mental patients.

Four years ago, I was asked to consult with Thomas and his family in the north of France. Thomas was at the time a 20-year-old young man, and was an only child. He had been diagnosed at birth with testicular agenesis, a rare and debilitating illness that, because of a severe hormonal imbalance, manifests in marked feminine traits, creating, during Thomas' childhood and adolescence, intolerable relational problems at school and with his peers. Repeated episodes of bullying forced Thomas to abandon school prematurely. From the age of 12, he had been in and out of psychiatric hospitals, and by the age of 20 had spent almost half of his life in hospital. Thomas had been labelled with an inordinately large number of diagnoses over time: schizophrenia, borderline personality disorder, bipolar disorder, eating disorder, etc. Each diagnosis was accompanied by frequent changes in medications, including electro-convulsive therapy. The parents were simple people, living in a small village in Normandy, and seemed to have lost hope in their son's recovery, and even more so, in his psychiatric treatment. The mother took care of all of Thomas's needs but she was over-protective, and treated him as a small and immature child. His most recent psychiatrist had seen the young man mainly individually, and occasionally with the parents. He suggested the consultation with myself, hoping to get some new, more helpful directions.

I cannot go into a detailed description of the session and I will limit myself to reporting two or three basic therapeutic interventions. The first intervention, prior to the consultation, concerned the manner I presented myself in therapy. I did not want to present myself as a powerful psychiatrist/family therapist, and I chose, on purpose, to speak in the session using my limited knowledge of French, without using the services of a translator, as I do in many other circumstances. I wanted to be humble and to elicit the expertise of the family instead. I entered the room with a French dictionary in my hands. I took a piece of paper, and placed it on the table at the centre of the room. I started the session by asking Thomas to write down something positive about himself, a question that was as unusual as it was unexpected for both him and his parents, who were more accustomed to discussing his failings and illnesses. After a lengthy wait and much warm encouragement on my part, Thomas, very surprised, started to list some of his positive traits: generosity, creativity, altruism, which were gradually confirmed by the parents, who were equally stunned by a psychiatrist who asked such unusual, and seemingly unimportant, questions. This exercise transformed the context of the session and all three were noticeably relieved, as the positive aspects of Thomas facilitated the family linking together. This was in such direct contrast to their usual sense of shame and sorrow around Thomas' psychiatric condition. The very purpose behind my question was my desire to challenge the family's profound sense of hopelessness.

Having established a close alliance with the young man through his listing of his positive qualities, I asked him to move from sitting between his parents to sit next to me. When Thomas sat between his parents, he regressed to appear as a six-year-old child, looking at his mother for confirmation whenever he wanted to talk. While Thomas looked and acted like a small child when seated between his parents, his behaviour became much more mature once he moved out from that space, both physically and metaphorically. I started to engage him as an adult, and to explore the story of his parents' upbringing. For the first time in his life, he was recognized and listened to as a grown-up man by his parents, who had difficulties believing that their son was so interested and well informed about their personal life stories.

Both parents had carried heavy responsibilities and duties in their families of origin, long before the birth of their son, who arrived after many years of marriage and reproductive difficulties. The mother had an alcoholic father and a totally incapacitated mother, and from the age of ten, had been responsible for her siblings. I understood that the mother had been in charge of everyone's problems from an early age, and that this function had been maintained throughout her life. Besides Thomas' issues, she also took care of her husband, constantly supporting him to cope with his depressive moods. Thomas' father, who was sad and withdrawn throughout the whole session, was brought up in a family shackled to their work in the fields, and by the unresolved grief for the premature loss of two baby sisters, one before his birth and the other a few years later. The father appeared to be buried as much as his two deceased siblings, without having much voice or impetus for initiative in his current family.

It was amazing to notice, once more in this session, the power of giving words and meanings to family distortions and individual suffering, taken out of the context of blame and sorrow. Revisiting family history and uncovering issues from the past allowed for more opening in the present. In naming the mother as a "professional helper", the mother was given permission to try to change her role of a chronic helper, and allow other people to support her. Giving voice to the father's buried grief and loss allowed the father to start to deal with his own depression for the early losses in his life, and learn to assume more personal power. Reframing Thomas in a positive light instilled hope in Thomas and his family that he could heal and recover and enter mainstream society. Freeing Thomas from being the focus of family worry allowed the parental couple to feel more alive. In working with the "we-ness" of the family as a healing unit, the family became activated, which paved the way for transformation.

I found it remarkable that Thomas' mental faculties were still intact and well-functioning, in spite of him having spent almost half of his life in hospital. This assessment gave me the impetus to suggest the need for Thomas to find a job and move out of the family home, thereby creating some much-needed distance from both his parents and from the hospital. The successful implementation of this project required the ongoing commitment and support of his psychiatrist, the first practitioner who was interested in him and his parents as a family. I myself was very impressed by the incredibly positive effect of this meeting on the whole family, but I was uncertain about the future. As a young psychiatrist, I had been warned by older professionals against miraculous endings, and aware of the danger of "flying into health" with the possibilities of serious relapses. However, I have always challenged the prejudicial assumption that the lives of chronic disease patients and their helpless families were inevitably doomed. After injecting hope and empowering family members in therapy, I like to keep the position of "wait and see".

Just over a year later, I received a note from the psychiatrist, who had continued to meet with the family for several months, in which he informed me that Thomas was now living in an apartment in a small town 15 kilometers from his parents, with whom his relationship had much improved. Moreover, he had secured a part-time job at the local Impressionist Museum. In his note, he told me that the family had a very fond memory of the consultation, and that they would be very glad to meet with me again, if I ever came back to France, "to show me how Thomas had changed". On my return to Paris for a family therapy seminar a year later, I invited the family and their psychiatrist to a follow-up session. In spite of many years of clinical experience, I could not believe my eyes. The changes in Thomas were evident not only in his manner and way of speaking, but also in his new positive attitude to life. Father looked much more alive and mother appeared more relaxed, and both parents seemed to have finally come out of a nightmare lasting

20 years and were even able to think of themselves as a couple, after many years of emotional distance. The following year again I had contact with Thomas, this time by phone. The psychiatrist told me how much Thomas had wanted to speak with me and, during the phone conversation, Thomas expressed his regret at not having been able to return to Paris to meet with me because he was too busy with work! At the same time, he confirmed that his parents were doing things together that he would never have imagined. Again, in November of last year, I was back in Paris, and this time I had a Skype conversation with Thomas in front of the numerous attendees at my workshop. I invited him to visit me in Australia some day in the future to meet the kangaroos, and I asked him to send pictures of him working at the museum. He was very moved over the phone, and many professionals who have heard of his story of personal renewal and happiness have echoed this feeling. The parents also sent me a long letter in which they described their second life as parents and as a couple.

These long and intense journeys with families in distress, who have been able to shift from suffering and grief to hope and new positive experiences, have enriched my professional life and given me a profound appreciation of these therapeutic encounters, which go beyond professional performance and success. Thomas and the many other problematic people – children as well as adults – described in this book, through their capacity to transform and heal together with their families, have been an extraordinary opportunity and a special gift to activate the most human and spiritual dimension of myself in order to connect emotionally with them through caring and love. I hope this book, through the many examples reported, will help therapists to be fully themselves and discover the true art of therapy.

References

American Psychiatric Association (1994). *Diagnostic and Statistical Manual of Mental Disorders,* 4th ed. (DSM-IV). Arlington, VA: American Psychiatric Association.

American Psychiatric Association (2013). *Diagnostic and Statistical Manual of Mental Disorders,* 5th ed. (DSM-5). Arlington, VA: American Psychiatric Association.

Andolfi, M. & Mascellani, A. (2013). *Teen Voices. Tales of Family Therapy.* San Diego: Wisdom Moon Publishing.

Andolfi, M., Angelo, C. & de Nichilo, M. (1989). *The Myth of Atlas: Families and the Therapeutic Story.* New York: Brunner/Mazel.

Andolfi, M., Angelo, C. & D'Atena, P. (2001). *La Terapia Narrata dalle Famiglie.* Milan: Raffaello Cortina.

Breunlin, D., Pinsof, W. & Russell, W. (2011). Integrative Problem Centered Meta-frameworks Therapy: Core Concepts and Hypothesizing. *Family Process,* 50, 293–313.

Carr, A. (2009a). The Effectiveness of Family Therapy and Systemic Interventions for Child-focused Problems. *Journal of Family Therapy,* 31(1), 3–45.

Carr, A. (2009b). The Effectiveness of Family Therapy and Systemic Interventions for Adult-focused Problems. *Journal of Family Therapy,* 31(1), 46–74.

Duncan, B., Miller, S. & Sparks, A. (2000). *The Heroic Client: A Revolutionary Way to Improve Effectiveness Through Client-directed, Outcome-informed Therapy.* San Francisco: Jossey-Bass.

Fivaz-Depeursinge, E. & Corboz-Warnery, A. (1999). *The Primary Triangle: a Developmental Systems View of Mothers, Fathers, Infants*. New York: Basic Books.

Fivaz-Depeursinge, E. & Philipp, D. (2014). *The Baby and the Couple: Understanding and Treating Young Families*. London: Routledge.

Frances, A. (2013). *Essentials of Psychiatric Diagnosis, Revised Edition: Responding to the Challenge of DSM 5*. New York: Guilford Press.

Friedlander, M., Escudero, V. & Heatherington, L. (2005). *Therapeutic Alliances with Couples and Families: An Empirical Informed Guide to Practice*. Washington, DC: American Psychological Association Books.

Pinsof, W. (1995). *Integrative Problem Centered Therapy*. New York: Basic Books.

Pinsof, W. & Greenberg, L. (Eds.) (1986). *The Psychotherapeutic Process: A Research Handbook*. New York: Guilford Press.

Pinsof, W. & Wynne, L. (2000). Toward Progress Research. Closing the Gap Between Family Therapy Practice and Research. *Journal of Marital and Family Therapy*, 26, 1–8.

Sexton, T. & Datchi, C. (2014). The Development and Evolution of Family Therapy Research: Its Impact on Practice, Current Status and Future Directions. *Family Process*, 53(3), 415–433.

INDEX

abandonment 20, 30
Accademia di Psicoterapia della Famiglia 46
access, level of 63–64
Ackerman Family Therapy Institute 47
Ackerman, N. W. 5, 6
adolescents: adoptive families 30, 31;
  assessment 56; changing refusal to
  collaboration 109; family life cycle
  10; listening to 131; physical contact
  119–120; siblings 64; therapist's active
  movements 106; verbal expressions of 84
adoptive families 29–31, 63
adulthood, transition to 10
affective attunement 98, 112, 114
Aldous, J. 11
American Psychological Association 34
Andolfi, M. 6, 41, 43
Angelo, C. 6
anorexia 69, 79, 85–86, 124
anxiety 17, 18, 28
"as if" questions 91–92
assessment 56–57, 60–61, 63–64
attachment 59, 61, 121
attentive listening 72
authority, personal 13–14
autonomy 13, 58

Bank, S. P. 63
Barreto, A. 78
Bateson, G. 2, 5, 53
Beavin, J. H. 4, 82, 113
bedwetting 69
belonging 18–19, 58

bereavement 80, 114–116, 125, 129
Bertrando, P. 83
Birdwhistell, R. L. 96
birth 10, 11, 41, 61–62
blended families 26–28, 64
body language see non-verbal
  communication
Bonvicini, M. L. 32
boomerang generation 10
Borda, C. 72
Borg, S. 97
Boscolo, L. 41
Boszormenyi-Nagy, I. 4, 5, 12–13
boundaries 57, 100, 118
Bowen, Murray 4, 6; couple therapy 112;
  differentiation of self 5, 17–18, 19;
  family genograms 5, 43; therapist as
  coach 105; triangles 39
Brief Focused Therapy 87, 133
Byng-Hall, J. 43

Caillé, P. 48
camouflaged couple therapy 62
Carr, A. 134
Carter, E. A. 10
case examples 124–129, 136–139;
  adoptive families 31; changing refusal to
  collaboration 109; chronic child 20–21;
  couple therapy 62, 63; death of a child
  114–116; directness 74–75; elective
  mutism 116; family myths 14–17;
  family resentment 108; genograms
  44–46; information provision 85–86;

inter-generational questions 94; joining
73; locked door metaphor 88, 92–93;
physical contact 118–119, 120, 121,
122–124; relational questions 91;
relational statements 88–89; rituals
79–80; role-play 52–53; rules of the game
108–109; sculpture 49–50; tears 105
causality 2, 83
Cecchin, G. 41
change 3, 10–11, 12, 114
children: adoptive families 29–31;
assessment 56; being truthful with
74–75; blended families 27–28; as
co-therapists 68–69; communicating
with 82; cross-cultural families 32; death
of a child 114–116; eye contact 104;
family life cycle 10; genograms 44–45;
high-conflict couples 62; homosexual
parents 35–36; leaving home 10, 11, 41,
60; listening to 131; migrant families
33; physical contact 117, 118, 119–120,
121; playful language 84, 101; playing
with toys 76–77; relational questions 90;
Rob's burdens case example 124–129;
role-play 52–53; sculpture 48–49; seating
arrangements in therapy 102–103;
single-parent families 25–26; temporal
jumps 93–94; therapeutic alliance 66;
therapist's active movements 106;
three-storey house metaphor 57;
triangulation 40–41; see also siblings
chronic child 19–21
circularity 6
Cirillo, S. 40–41
coaching 18
collaborative therapies 6
communication 2–3, 4, 6, 82–83; see also
language; non-verbal communication;
silence
comparison questions 90–91
Compernolle, T. 82
"conductors" 6
confidentiality 133
conflict 25, 31, 76–77; high-conflict
couples 58–59, 60, 61, 62; relational
questions 90; therapist's silence 113
constructivism 6, 67
context 3, 87
context shadows 70
contracts, therapeutic 108
conversational therapy 83
Cook, M. 98
Corboz-Warnery, A. 99, 134
counter-transference 70–71

couples 9; assessment 56, 60–61; chronic
child 19, 20–21; communicating with
82–83; configurations 57–58; de facto
relationships 28–29; doormat metaphor
78–79; family life cycle 10; follow-up
research 136; harmonious 58, 60,
61–62; high-conflict 58–59, 60, 61, 62;
influence of parents 20, 21; information
provided by 84–85; inter-generational
questions 94; loyalties 13; migrants
31, 32–34; mixed 31–32; non-verbal
communication 103; pauses for
reflection 111–112; relational questions
89–90, 91; role-play 52, 53; rules of the
game 108–109; same-sex 28, 29, 34–36;
"sandwiched" 59–60; sculpture 49–50;
therapeutic alliance 66; three-storey
house metaphor 57; unstable 59, 62–63;
see also marriage
cross-cultural families 31–32
Crouch, S. 36
crowded-nest syndrome 10, 60
cultural family therapy 19
culture: communication 82; cross-cultural
families 31–32; cultural norms 12; eye
contact 97; migrant families 32–34;
non-verbal communication 97;
"professional handicaps" 51–52;
therapeutic alliance 107
curiosity 72, 74, 75–76, 84, 86, 104, 107

Datchi, C. 134
de facto relationships 28–29
de-labeling 68
death 10, 79–80, 106
"debts" 13
dependence 20, 58–59
depression 12, 28, 44, 45, 69, 103, 105,
138
Di Nicola, V. F. 116
*Diagnostic and Statistical Manual of Mental
Disorders* (DSM-5) 34, 131–132
dialogic-didactic method 83
differentiation 5, 17–18, 19, 35, 42, 57–58,
67–68; see also individuation
direct questions 90
directness 73–75
divorce 11, 25–26, 79
doormat metaphor 78–79
Double-bind Theory 2–3
dramatization 48, 52, 53, 78
Duncan, B. 134
duties 13
dyadic relationships 2, 17

Ekman, P. 98, 104
elderly care 59–60
elective mutism 116
emotional cut-off 19, 58
emotional functioning 18
emotions: attentive listening by therapist
72; eye contact 97, 104; facial
expressions 97–98; genograms 43;
kinaesthetic behaviour 97; lung language
102; posture 98–99; relational questions
89; role-play 53; sculpture 47, 48, 50;
therapist's role 71
empathy 72, 77, 89, 97, 121
empty-nest syndrome 11, 60
encopresis 69, 70
Epston, D. 78, 87
Erickson, Milton 3, 87
Escudero, V. 134
extended family 33
extra-marital relationships 61, 62
eye contact 73, 89, 97, 101–104

facial expressions 97–98, 104
failure 72
Family Association of the Mentally Ill 2,
132
family career concept 11
family genograms 5, 18, 42–47, 50–51, 69,
79, 108
family life cycle 9–11, 14, 78
"family mandates" 64
family sculpture 47–52, 105–106, 118, 135
Family Systems Theory 17–18
family therapy, effectiveness of 132–134
fathers: absent 20–21; blended families 27;
Bowen's theory 17; death of 125, 129;
family myths 16; rituals 79–80, 106;
sculpture 48–49; single-parent families
25, 26; see also parents
favouritism 27, 40, 63
fears 42, 50, 79–80, 106, 122, 135
Ferenczi, S. 117
Ferreira, A. J. 14
Fish, R. 4
Fivaz-Depeursinge, E. 99, 134
follow-up 134–136
Framo, J. L. 4, 5, 6
Frances, A. 132
Freud, Sigmund 117
Freudian method 7
Friedlander, M. 134
friendships 60
Friesen, W. V. 98
Fromm, Erich 1

gender 82–83, 100, 107
genealogy 42–43
General Systems Theory 1
genograms 5, 18, 42–47, 50–51, 69, 79,
108
Gerson, R. 43
gestures 73, 98, 108
Goff, J. K. 13
Goldenberg, H. 13
Goldenberg, I. 13
Golombok, S. 24, 36
grandparents 10, 41–42, 59, 89
Greenberg, L. 133–134
grief 10, 79–80, 104–105, 114–116, 129,
137–138, 139
Guerin, P. J. 43

Haber, R. 118
haemophilia 74
Haley, J.: divergence in therapy approaches
6; perverse triad 3, 40; role-play 53;
Strategic Therapy 87; supervision by
69–70; systemic-cybernetic perspective 2
Hall, E. T. 99, 100
harmonious couples 58, 60, 61–62
Heatherington, L. 134
Hellinger, B. 43
high-conflict couples 58–59, 60, 61, 62
Hoffman, L. 6
homeostasis 2, 3
homosexual couples 28, 29, 34–36
Horney, Karen 1
hospital settings 68
humour 75, 77–78, 119
hypothesis formulation 83–84
hypothetical questions 91–92

"I position" 14, 19
identity 34
images 78
immaturity 5, 18, 19
implicit relational knowledge 7
impotence 72
indirect questions 90
individuation 13, 18, 35, 58; see also
differentiation
information 84–86
instigation 40–41
inter-generational intimidation 13–14, 20
inter-generational questions 93–94
inter-subjective consciousness 7
intimate distance 99
intimidation 13–14, 20
inverted funnel metaphor 85

Jackson, D. D. 2, 53, 82, 113
Johnson, S. M. 61
joining 72–73, 133

Kahn, M. D. 63
Keeney, B. P. 87–88
Kendon, A. 96
kinesics 96
knowledge 7

La Sala, M. 35
language 75–76, 82–95, 119; foundations
    of therapeutic dialogue 83–85;
    gathering and selection of information
    85–86; lung language 102; reframing
    86–88; relational questions 89–94;
    relational statements 88–89; *see
    also* communication; non-verbal
    communication
Laperriere, Kitty 47
laughter 77–78, 104
Lausanne Triadic Play 99, 134
leaving home 10, 11, 41, 60
lesbians 35
life cycle 9–11, 14, 78
listening 72, 73, 111–112, 113–114, 131
locked door metaphor 88, 92–93
loneliness 28, 49
loss 30, 79, 105, 129
loyalties 5, 12–13, 42; blended families 27;
    migrant families 33–34; siblings 63–64
lung language 102

marriage 13, 56; arranged 32; crisis in the
    institution of 28–29; *see also* couples
maturity 18, 20, 21
McGoldrick, M. 10, 43
Medical Model 2, 39, 63, 68, 83, 131–132
medication 73, 132, 136
memory 106
men: inter-generational values 42;
    single-person families 28; stereotypes
    about 117; therapeutic alliance 107; *see
    also* fathers
Menninger, K. 117
Mental Research Institute, Palo Alto 2, 3,
    4, 53
metaphors 76, 92, 103
migrant families 31, 32–34
Milan school 4, 6, 78, 83, 84, 87
Miller, S. 134
Minuchin, S. 1, 3, 4, 6, 57; critique of
    systemic-cybernetic perspective 5;
    joining 72; multi-generational family

therapy 5; narrative therapy 67;
    parentification 41; sibling relationship
    63; triangulation 17, 40
mixed couples 31–32
Montagano, S. 43
Montagu, A. 121
Moreno, J. L. 52
mothers: Bowen's theory 17; demanding
    21; estrangement from 122–123; facial
    expressions 98; family myths 16;
    lesbians 35; listening to 73; Rob's
    burdens case example 125–129;
    sculpture 49; single-parent families 25;
    suicide 74–75; *see also* parents
mourning 10
movement 104–109
multi-generational family therapy 4–5, 64,
    84, 86, 93–94
multi-partiality 84
myths 5, 9, 12, 14–17, 20, 42, 78

names 12
narrative, multi-generational 11–12
narrative therapy 67, 78, 83, 87
neglect 63
Neo-Freudian theories 1
network therapy approach 78
neuroscience 132
neutrality 4, 83, 84
non-verbal communication (body
    language) 3, 82, 96–110, 119; body
    spacing and relational boundaries
    99–100; eye contact 73, 89, 97,
    101–104; facial expressions 97–98, 104;
    follow-up research 135; gestures 73, 98,
    108; movement 104–109; paralinguistic
    system 100–101; posture 98–99;
    relational questions 89; sculpture 47, 48,
    50, 52; *see also* physical contact; silence
norms 12, 14
nuclear family 24

objects: metaphorical 135; physical contact
    through 120–121; playing with 76
observation 6–7, 39–55, 56; eye contact
    103–104; genograms 42–47; role-play
    52–53; triad as basic unit of 39–42
older people 28, 59–60
Onnis, L. 48

Palazzoli, Selvini 4
Palo Alto Mental Research Institute 2, 3,
    4, 53
Papp, Peggy 47

paralinguistic system 100–101
parental alienation syndrome 40
parentification 41, 63
parents: adoptive families 29–31; blaming
 of 2–3, 132; blended families 26–28;
 changing roles 13; collaboration
 with 69; cross-cultural 32; *de facto*
 relationships 28–29; directness 74–75;
 estrangement from 122–124; family
 forms 24; genograms 44; homosexuality
 35–36; information provided by 85–86;
 intimidation by 13–14, 20; locked door
 metaphor 92–93; relational questions 90;
 ritual of divorce 79; sculpture 48; seating
 arrangements in therapy 102–103;
 single-parent families 25–26; standing
 up to 19, 21; temporal jumps 93–94;
 therapeutic alliance 66; Thomas' case
 example 137–139; three-storey house
 metaphor 57; triangulation 40–41; *see
 also* fathers; mothers
partial truth 84
pathology 2
patriarchal family 24
pauses 111–112
Pazzagli, A. 43
Pendagast, E. G. 43
personal authority 13–14
personal distance 99
personality 98
perverse triad 3, 40
pharmaceuticals 132
Philipp, D. 134
photos 45–46, 47
physical contact 99, 100, 103, 107,
 116–124
Pinsof, W. 133–134
play 69, 75; Lausanne Triadic Play 99, 134
playfulness 75–77, 79
posture 98–99
pragmatics of communication 4
Prata, G. 41
problem redefinition 87
"professional handicaps" 51–52
projections 67
provocation 74, 77
proximity 99, 103, 107–108
psychiatry 131, 132
psychoanalysis 4, 7, 39, 71, 83; lack of
 evaluation 133; physical contact 117;
 seating arrangements 103; silence 112
psychodrama 52
psychodynamic approaches 40, 96–97, 132
psychopathology 39, 44, 57, 68, 83, 132

psychosocial orphans 59
psychosomatic symptoms 28, 52, 62, 70,
 94, 131
public distance 99–100
puzzle metaphor 86

questioning: circular 3, 83; relational
 questions 89–94

reciprocity 20
reconciliation 48, 79, 116
reflection 111–112
reframing 68–69, 85, 86–88, 107, 138
refusal 109
regression 49, 137
Reich, W. 117
Reiter M. D. 72
rejection 49, 50
relational deceit 40–41
Relational Psychology 1, 19, 42
relational questions 89–94
relational skills 71–78
relational statements 88–89
remarriage 27, 79
resilience 77
rhythm of voice 101
rituals 10, 14, 78–80, 105–106, 124
Rodgers, R. 11
Rogers, Carl 111
role-play 52–53, 105–106
role reversal 25
roles 12, 14, 15, 16, 64
Roustang, F. 71, 115
rules of the game 108–109

sadness 28, 89, 104, 105
same-sex couples 28, 29, 34–36
"sandwiched" couples 59–60
Satir, Virginia 6, 47, 53, 71, 103, 118
scapegoating 5, 67
Scheflen, A. E. 96–97, 99
schizophrenia 2–3
school phobia 69
scripts, inter-generational 11–12, 14, 48
sculpture 47–52, 105–106, 118, 135
seating arrangements 102–103
self: differentiation of 5, 17–18, 35, 67–68;
 inner self of therapist 69–71; relational
 questions 90; self-contact 100
self-disclosure 71, 117
self-esteem 13, 48
self-harm 120
self-reflection 51, 72, 77
Selvini, M. 40–41

Selvini Palazzoli, M. 40–41
separation: belonging and 18–19, 58; differentiation of self 17–18; family life cycle 10; homosexuality 35; marital 11, 25, 26–27, 41, 44
Sexton, T. 134
sexual contact 116
shared motivation 84
siblings: adoptive families 30–31; assessment 63–64; family myths 15; genograms 43, 44; harmonious couples 58; physical contact 120, 124; rivalry 27; seating arrangements in therapy 102
sighs 102
silence 72, 82, 96, 101, 104, 112–116
Simons, J. 70
single-parent families 25–26
single-person families 28
social constructionism 6, 67
social distance 99
social psychiatry 131, 132
social support 10
Socrates 83
SOFTA (System for Observing Family Therapy Alliance) 134
solidarity 33, 131
Sommer, R. 100
Sorrentino, A. M. 40–41
space 99–100, 107
Spark, G. 5, 12–13
Sparks, A. 134
step-families 26–28, 64
stereotypes 16, 31, 32, 117
Stern, D. N. 7, 98, 104–105, 112
stigma 36
Strategic Therapy 87
stress 10–11, 18, 94
subjectivity 4
suicide 74–75, 119
Sullivan, Harry Stack 1
supervision 50–51
symmetrical escalations 112
"system purists" 4, 6
systemic-cybernetic perspective 2, 3, 5, 6
systemic family therapy 53, 70, 83–84
systemic-relational approach 7, 43, 56, 72
Systems Theory 1–2, 3, 5, 82, 83, 84, 86

tears 104, 105
temporal jumps 5, 57, 93–94
Terri, A. K. 32
therapeutic alliance 6, 66–68; evaluation of the 133, 134; follow-up research 135; humour 77; movement 106–109;

physical contact 117, 119–121; relational statements 88; sculpture 48, 50
therapeutic contracts 108
therapeutic puzzle 86
therapeutic relationship 7, 67; evaluation of the 133; genograms 44; physical contact 117; quality of the 134; reframing 87; vital forms 105
therapists: active movements 106–107; eye contact 103–104; follow-up research 135–136; hypothesis formulation 83–84; inner self of 69–71; neutrality 4; observation by 6–7; pauses for reflection 111–112; physical contact 116–121; "professional handicaps" 51–52; relational skills 71–78; silence 112–116; therapist couples in consultation 53; training 46–47, 50–51
third planet 6, 67
Thompson, Clara 1
three-storey house metaphor 57
time 9, 11
Toffanetti, D. 83
Tomm, K. 83
tone of voice 89, 100–101, 111
touch see physical contact
toys, playing with 76–77
training 46–47, 50–51
transference 7, 117
transitions 10, 16
trauma 79–80, 117
tri-generational maps 5
tri-generational triangles 41–42, 67
triadic questions 89–90
triads 3, 39–42, 43, 67, 89
"triangling" 17
triangulation 17, 26, 27, 40–41, 63
Tronick, E. Z. 98
trust: body spacing 99; damaged by extra-marital relationships 61; family rituals 79; inter-generational questions 93; joining 73; lack of 60, 75; mutual trust in couples 36; physical contact 117–118

University of Rome 46
unstable couples 59, 62–63

values 9, 12, 14, 24, 32, 42
violence: adopted children 30–31; domestic 48, 69, 114, 117, 123; physical contact 118
visual empathy 97
vital dynamics 104, 105, 111
Volker, T. 32

Von Bertalanffy, L. 1, 5
Von Foerster, H. 6

Walsh, F. 10
Watzlawick, P.: context 3; human
    communication 4, 5, 82; silence 113; as
    "system purist" 6; systemic-cybernetic
    perspective 2
Weakland, J. 2, 4, 6, 53
Wetchler J. 32
Whitaker, C. A. 4, 6; counter-transference
    70–71; couple formation 56; humour
    77; hypothesis formulation 84;
    metaphorization 92; multi-generational
    family therapy 5; seating arrangements 103

White, M. 78, 87
Williamson, D. S. 13–14, 20
"wish sculptures" 106
women: family myths 15; inter-
    generational values 42; lesbians 35;
    single-person families 28; stereotypes 16;
    therapeutic alliance 107; *see also* mothers
words, playing with 75–76
work 61
Wynne, L. 134

Yalom, I. D. 118–119

Zappella, M. 118
Zur, O. 118